A global community book project

Passion over Past

Transforming the world together, one testimony at a time.

Laska Paré

PASSION OVER PAST, A global community book project, transforming the world together, one testimony at a time.

By Laska Paré

Originally Published in Toronto, Ontario, Canada

Copyright © 2015 by Ms. Laska Paré

All Rights Reserved

ISBN-10: 1508901740
ISBN-13: 978-1508901747

All rights reserved. No Part of this book may be used or reproduced in any manner whatsoever, stored in a retrieval system, or transmitted in any form or by any means, electronic or mechanical, including photocopying or recording without the written permission of the author or publisher, except in the case of brief quotations embodied in critical articles and review. For information, contact Passion over Past, Toronto, Ontario, Canada at: passionoverpast@yahoo.ca

The insightful content of this book is designed to provide helpful information on the subject discussed. This book is not meant to be used, nor should it be used, to diagnose or treat any medical or psychological condition. For diagnosis or treatment of any medical problems consult with a physician. The publisher and author are not responsible for any specific health needs that may require medical supervision and are not liable for any damages or negative consequences from any treatment, action, application or preparation, to any person reading or following the information in this book. The testimonies portrayed in this book are true, but names and specific details may have been changed to maintain the participants privacy.

To all those I encountered on my journey – Thank you for your kindness, generosity, support and love.

My gratitude is beyond words.

Contents

Foreword..vi
Preface..x

Passion over Past...1
  ~ Andrea Glew ~..2
  ~ Anonymous ~..6
  ~ Elisha Cook ~.......................................10
  ~ T. Hossain ~..12
  ~ Yvonne Scully ~.....................................16
  ~ Samira ElAtia ~.....................................19
  ~ Daria Brown ~.......................................25
  ~ Pina ~..26
  ~ Katelyn Butler-Birmingham ~.........................29
  ~ Lucy Sanford ~......................................32
  ~ Magdalena H Brzoska ~...............................40
  ~ Jasmine ~...45
  ~ Charlene Guzzo ~....................................52
  ~ Katarina MacLeod ~..................................55
  ~ April McIntyre ~....................................59
  ~ Esther Kim ~..60
  ~ Raha Sabet Sarvestany ~.............................67

~ Alena Dervisevic ~ 73
~ Stephanie McLean ~ 74
~ Sachi* ~ 78
~ Kelly McNamara ~ 84
~ Anonymous ~ 88
~ Hanna ~ 91
~ Su Tran ~ 94
~ Laska Paré ~ 99

The Power of Choice 103
   The Seven Day Commitment Challenge 110
The Power of Testimony 122
   The Guidelines 126
Closing Thoughts 128

About the Author 130
Additional Information 131
Acknowledgments 133

Foreword

> *There are two ways to live: you can live as if nothing is a miracle; you can live as if everything is a miracle.* - Albert Einstein

mir•a•cle - noun: miracle; plural noun: miracles

* A highly improbable or extraordinary event, development, or accomplishment that brings very welcome consequences.

I believe that life is a miracle, but our choices, and our 'stories', can cause the experience of that miracle to become a beautiful dream or an unforgettable nightmare. I have traveled the globe working, mentoring or speaking with individuals and groups for over 20 years, following my dreams. By living my life passionately I have always done what I love, made choices others thought to be crazy, and lived life by my own terms. I chose to align my 'stories' with the understanding that life is an education. I have laughed when tripping up stairs, cried during movies with happy ends and smiled at strangers on the street – which confuses a lot of people. But these are all choices I make everyday; choices that allow me to enjoy my life no matter what my experiences are. This is *'The Power of Choice'* and Laska Paré explains the effects of these choices in a simple and powerful way in her book, *Passion over Past*.

Laska is the second child of my older brother and she was born and raised in small town Strathroy, Ontario. Laska was a fun and happy sibling to 2 younger brothers and an older sister – always supportive and assisting in the household and in her community. Even after the death of her mother in a tragic accident when she was only 13, she continued to deal with life positively. She went on to get a Visual Arts and Communications degree, with a minor in French, and a Masters degree in Communication, specializing in government relations. But after a professor in university sexually harassed her, her life fell apart and depression followed. Then one day Laska started to run to cope with her experience. The running did not transform her life, but it did bring her smack in the face with *The Power of Choice*. And through this new understanding she could choose to 'be' someone other than a victim. When Laska started sharing her experiences she realized *The Power of Testimony*, and how this connectedness to her community could assist others in transforming their lives too. Thus the book Passion over Past was born and she began a new life, with a new purpose.

Although in this book Laska has chosen to focus on women's testimonies, and how Choice and Testimony can transform one's life, I have shared excerpts from her book with several male clients and friends – all of whom had profound breakthroughs in their own lives as a result. Laska makes understanding this information and these new ideas very simplistic and her *Seven Day Commitment Challenge* allows everyone to start their own transformative process immediately. I believe community is the answer to many of this world's social problems as connection and a sense of belonging are universal and desired by all of humanity. Passion over Past starts the conversation with understanding our differences, developing tolerance and celebrating our experiences; this is the path to freedom of mind and spirit. Everyone will benefit from this book while getting to know the women involved in this project from their testimonies.

I am so proud of my niece and her passion for life, community and humanity. This except from Jasmine's testimony in *Passion over Past*, sums it all up…

"After meeting Laska Paré at work one day, I changed for good. Laska added happiness, hope and confidence to my life. Just looking at her exuberant character, contagious sense of kindness, and loving spirit of life makes you truly understand that anything is possible! It also presents you with a moment of reflection of how important it is to be kind to everyone you meet, because you don't know anyone's battles, and you have absolutely no idea how you may impact their life."

Remember where you are right now, because Passion over Past will forever change your life. As Laska always says, *'If you are passionate and committed, anything is possible'* and life will always be experienced as a miracle.

Live life happy, and always make passionate choices...

Christian Paré

*Co-Founder Nations United Inc.
International Mentor, Speaker and Humanitarian
Author, Editor & Lifestyle Coach
Toronto, ON, Canada*

Preface

I discovered running as a result of a sexual harassment experience in university. The strength and confidence I gained through running provided me the opportunity to see myself, and the context in which I exist, in a completely new light. Ultimately, this led to me turning my life around with passion! Running, however, did not transform my life; rather it empowered my understanding of choice. By choosing to run, I instantly transitioned from Victim to Athlete, which resulted in a complete life transformation. By living passionately and being committed to my choices, I learned that anything is possible! I furthered my athletic abilities, quickly shifting from running to Ultra running which led to a world of possibilities I never foresaw for myself. By understanding the power of my choices (*The Power of Choice*) and the power of my testimony (*The Power of Testimony*) I produced unimaginable results in my life! Not only did I want to share my discovery of this understanding with the world, I wanted to create a platform that would inspire, empower and equip others to produce unimaginable results in their life. My vision took shape in the form of a book, and the project *Passion over Past* was born!

Passion over Past (P>P) is a global community book project that stands for transforming the world together, one testimony at a time. I believe when we use our power collectively we can create lasting, positive change. As such, P>P consists of compelling self-written testimonies from women all over the world, who have experienced 'difficulty' because they were victims of abuse or they encountered a challenging life experience. While the women's testimonies detail the hardships they endured and struggles they faced, the point of empowerment stems from their moment of realization – the moment when they realized they could 'choose to be' powerful in spite of their past experiences. P>P highlights the transformative results you can produce when you choose to recognize that all experiences in your life are valuable and an important part of your journey; as such, your testimony is your greatest asset and can be utilized to transform our world.

I believe with proper understanding of *The Power of Choice* and *The Power of Testimony* anything is possible, which includes the unimaginable! As such, this book was designed to assist you in developing this understanding, first through reading the women's testimonies, which will empower you to take that first step and begin the process of living passionately over your past. And second, by completing *The Seven-Day Commitment Challenge* and following *The Guidelines*, which will equip you with the tools to build an extraordinary life for yourself, your family and others.

I am thrilled, honoured and excited to share this collective book project which includes testimonies, poems, quotes, words of wisdom and photographic work from women all over the world and from all walks of life. May you be inspired and empowered by those who have chosen to live passionately over their past!

Passion over Past

Transforming the world together, one testimony at a time.

When I was 28 I found myself in Pune, India after six months of travelling in Thailand and India with friends. At this point my friends had returned to their countries and I was on my own for the first time in a long while. This journey began when ten months previously I lost my boyfriend suddenly in a motorcycle accident. It was a journey of healing. I felt very vulnerable during this time and even more so because I was on my own when I arrived in Pune. The previous months had been a roller coaster of emotions and I planned to spend six months or more at the Osho Ashram in Pune to continue my healing journey. Needless to say, I was both excited and scared at the same time.

I arrived in Pune early afternoon by train and decided to check into a hotel for the night before going to the ashram the next day. After a shower and walk, I found a restaurant and sat down. The restaurant was quiet as it was a bit early, but everything on the menu sounded so good. When the waiter came over I ordered a chai and asked for a few more minutes with the menu. Seconds later, a middle aged Indian man in a business suit approached my table. He smiled and asked me where I was from. After a few minutes of chat, he ended up joining me for dinner. He seemed nice, ignoring the strange feeling in my stomach. "I'm just hungry" I thought. We sat for an hour or so eating and chatting about Canada, India, food, life, etc. When the bill came he insisted on paying, I thanked him. I told him I was going back to my hotel and when I said the name of the hotel, he exclaimed with surprise that his brother-in-law owned the hotel, what are the chances. I found this a bit of an odd coincidence and started to feel uncomfortable, but brushed it off as nothing. Back at the hotel lobby I thanked him again for dinner, said goodbye and headed to my room. As I approached the door of my room and put my key in the lock, I sensed someone behind me. As I opened my door, the man from the restaurant suddenly pushed his way in behind me. I yelled at him to get out but he grabbed my shoulders and pulled me to him. His lips were suddenly on mine, and his hands were going down my back... I shoved him away as hard as I could and started yelling for him to GET OUT! Fortunately we were close to the door so I shoved him again out into the hallway and slammed the door shut bolting it from the inside. I was shaking all over, tears running down my face, and completely undone.

The second the sun came up the next day I was already packed and ready to go. I got in the first rickshaw and went straight to the ashram. There were lots of other foreigners at the ashram, which made me feel safer and more comfortable for some reason. The ashram is a beautiful and peaceful place, which also helped. An American guy started talking to me. As we were chatting I suddenly burst into tears. I ended up telling him the whole story. He was very supportive and a good listener. I started to question myself while retelling the story. Did I do something to provoke him? What did I do wrong? How did I let this happen?

As I was telling the story to him, I realized that the man had followed me from the hotel. He had been in the lobby when I checked in but I didn't recognize him at the restaurant. I felt like a fool, sad, and very shaken up. But then I also remembered that I did have a 'funny feeling' when he approached the table, and it grew as the evening went on. My intuition was telling me something, and I didn't listen. The American guy was very kind and listened to my whole story. When I finished he said, "Always listen to that feeling in your stomach. It always knows the truth." Wise words.

For a while after that I blamed myself for not listening to my intuition and for putting myself in a dangerous situation. I questioned my ability to hear my inner self and my ability to 'read someone', especially men. These are traits that I previously prided myself on.

Fortunately I was in a place where healing was the focus. The people were there to help heal me and I was surrounded by a lot of love. I met some amazing people who helped me by listening and sharing similar experiences where they failed to listen to their intuition and learned from it. I did a lot of meditation, which really allowed me to connect with an inner silence and my intuitive being. I took a woman's tantra group, which helped me to connect to my oh-so-wise inner goddess self. I began to let go of my guilt for not seeing the situation for what it was and not listening to that inner knowing. There wasn't an exact moment where it all came together, but more of a process over time allowing me to understand that there is a 'small voice' that speaks to me, to all of us, and the more I practice listening to that voice, the more I can hear it. Once you can hear that voice of inner knowing, the truth becomes crystal clear. If I had listened to that first uneasy feeling I had in the restaurant, it would have ended there. And even though it was an awful and scary experience, I am grateful for it as it allowed me to have faith in that small voice and to learn how to better hear it. A process that continues today.

~ Andrea Glew ~

Like all people, I have faced challenges in my life. I have struggled with OCD (obsessive compulsive disorder), an anxiety related disorder, and with the stigma and misunderstandings associated with mental illness.

From a young age, my fearful reaction to 'normal' unwanted thoughts and my fear of dealing with normal, everyday, uncomfortable feelings eventually internalized and soon anxiousness and fear became part of my everyday experience. Over the years my illness roller coastered; at times it was non-existent and at others it was very intrusive – taking up many hours of the day. Getting to a point of self-awareness and changing thoughts and behaviors is challenging to say the least. It is a journey.

I did have the support and love of my family and friends, although they too are human, with limitations. Mental illness causes stress for everyone involved; the one who has it as well as their family and friends. Mostly, the greatest sadness that my mental illness has caused me has been the time that it has taken from my life, and also that my illness indirectly caused sadness in my family.

As well as struggling with an anxiety disorder I have also experienced its stigma. I have been misunderstood at times. That made the struggle worse. Some thought that I could just snap my fingers and stop being anxious. I have been laughed at and given strange looks. Some thought I was crazy. Some dehumanized me, thinking I was no longer worthy of dignity and respect. Those who behaved that way did so out of fear or ignorance. I don't hold grudges towards them. I realize that it takes dialoguing about the issues to bring about understanding and from there, compassion instead of judgement.

The truth I have always known is that I, like every other person in the world, have been created by God in His image and I am beautiful, strong, loving and loved. I am creative and intelligent. I am worthy of dignity. I am not greater or less than any other person. I am just me.

All people have challenges; some are more visible than others. They come in all kinds of disguises but the bottom line is that we are all human, and we all have mountains to climb in life. This commonality should unite us and allow us to be an inspiration to each other as we each overcome our obstacles and wake each day with hope.

I have always longed to be well. I hate that I have missed out on many moments in life and I hate that my family and I have experienced this pain. This is very sobering to me. But, I am also grateful that I have experienced this struggle; I feel it allowed me to focus on what is important in life as well as to be compassionate to others. My experience also has brought about a vulnerability and humility in me. Every life experience and how we respond to it helps shape our character.

I like this quote by C.S. Lewis,

> *"...Through suffering, we release our hold on the toys of this world, and know our true good lies in another world. We're like blocks of stone, out of which the sculptor carves the forms of men. The blows of his chisel, which hurt us so much, are what make us perfect. The suffering in this world is not the failure of God's love for us; it is that love in action."*

It is hard to name a dramatic turning point in my life because I see it more as a journey – like climbing a mountain. At times in my life I have been on the steep, tough climb and then I reach a plateau with a beautiful view and then around the corner there is another even steeper climb.

God and my faith, hope for the future, family love, and a passion for life, continue to sustain me.

Recently, through the support of my family I have been able to face this long struggle head on. My awareness of my challenges has matured and I have changed how I appraise and respond to previous stresses.

I am on my road to recovery and am doing well. I feel as if life has been breathed back into me. I feel alive and have so many hours in the day to live. I am grateful for the unconditional love of my family. I am grateful to my husband for his commitment and unconditional love. We are working through the entanglements that mental illness can bring to a marriage and family and it will take time, but we have hope and love.

One of the things that I find helpful is being present in each moment with whatever I am doing, to take my time and enjoy: work or pleasure. Everything we do, even the mundane things, have meaning and a ripple effect to those around us. When I am joyful, my family and others feel that joy radiated.

I can be there with and for my family and friends. I can be creative and use the gifts God has given me to live life to its fullest.

~ Anonymous ~

It is funny how powerful the mind is. I start by writing this, because my mind completely concealed the trauma that had occurred in my youth. For years I wondered why I had carried around shame and guilt despite my spirituality. Finally, I decided that to better my health and spiritual walk with God, I needed to address these prevalent toxins in my mind. As I began this exploration and renewal of my mind I felt stronger and more capable to be within myself. After doing this self-exploration, the incident from my youth revealed itself.

I was probably about 10 years old and was in for a routine check-up with my family doctor. My mother was in the room and simply thought the doctor was performing necessary testing. Unknowingly to her, the doctor molested me. While my pants were on and unzipped, he inserted his fingers into my vagina. My mother thought that he was palpating my lower stomach, as the pants concealed what his true motives were. This was not medically warranted and this was not right. For years I had struggled with self-perception and the thoughts in the back of my mind that I was unworthy, undeserving, shameful, guilty, and dirty. I did not understand why I feared men, and why intercourse with my husband brought on emotional and painful upsets. Now it all made sense.

Immediately, as my mind revealed the traumatic incident to me, a flood of emotions came over me. I was angry that someone who we should be able to trust would have done something like this. But I was grateful for the revived memory. I realized I had a choice. I could be bitter, resentful, hateful, and fitting myself within a label saying I was filthy, disgusting, unlovable, dirty, unclean, broken, or tainted. Or my other option was I could use this to strengthen me. I realized I could help others who had gone through the same thing, and I could label myself as strong, whole, healed, and a survivor. At this point in my life, I was studying to become a Naturopathic Doctor, and I realized that this incident was not revealed to me in order to bring me down, but to lift me up. This was an opportunity to help others who had walked this same path and struggled. Rather than burdening me, I would use this to fuel me.

If I had not drawn closer to my Lord and saviour Jesus Christ, and worked through the negative self-talk and thoughts, I honestly do not know how I would have walked through this. Although I am not okay with what happened to me, I am thankful for what working through this experience has brought me. No longer do the toxic thoughts that plagued my mind continue to reside. Instead I know who I am, what I can overcome with my faith, and the power of forgiveness. I am also thankful that the barrier that once separated myself and my husband, on an intimate level, is gone, and that I no longer feel ashamed or guilty.

Sisters and brothers, I encourage you, use your incident to strengthen you. You are a survivor. You are beautiful. You are not tainted, but whole. Embrace who you have become and who you will be.

~ Elisha Cook ~

Sixteen is when I came out to myself. I remember it was the night before Christmas; I sat on my bed, tears rolling down my eyes when I first gathered the courage to tell myself "I think I may be gay." I couldn't grasp what that meant for me. What would my life be like if I lived the way I felt inside? Really, the thought of being gay scared me. I prayed to God hoping that it is just a phase and I promised myself that I would do everything possible to not hurt my parents. I knew my life wouldn't be easy being South Asian, Muslim and gay. It's just not talked about in our culture.

Years passed by suppressing this very day. I went through university not telling anyone, but little did I realize how much this was eating away at me. I dated guys simply because I wanted to feel like I am part of a 'group'. I did everything possible to be 'normal', but inside I was numb. I created a picture in my head on how I wanted my life to be – married to a tall, handsome man, have a child and a successful career. That was my dream and I didn't want anyone to take it away from me, not even this thing called 'gay'.

At 22, I went into depression. With a university degree and without a job, living with the parents and still feeling gay, I was getting more and more lonely. I remember an entire summer locking myself up in my room.

25 is when I came out to my parents. It was 11pm at night when I picked up the phone and called my home. I was living in a different city by then. My hands were shaking, blood was rushing through my head and my heart was beating at light speed. Something hit me and I realized I

can't live my life in hiding. I can't pretend anymore. My mother picked up the phone and was eager to know how my day was. But all I wanted was to share the 9 years that I missed out with her, because I was gay. Tears were filing up my eyes, and I told my mother in my native language my secret. At first she could not comprehend what that meant. She grew up back home where talks of these were non-existent. She didn't know anyone who was gay. She only heard of it on the television. But after a brief pause, it hit her. She grew louder and louder on the phone and gave me an earful on the cliché reasons why being gay is wrong. I stopped her at one point and let her know, when I lived under the same roof with her and my dad, I felt lonely. Now that I live hundreds of kilometres away, this is the first time I feel close to her. This stopped her in her tracks, and she went quiet for a bit. Her tone changed and she asked me if I had my dinner. She told me to take care of myself, eat well and get a good sleep. She will talk to me tomorrow night again. That very moment, I realized that although she may not have accepted me, she is still my mother who cares about me.

The very next day, in the morning, I woke up with a big smile on my face. I went out and for the first time in a long while, I can honestly say I felt present and happy in this world.

None of this would have been possible, if I had let fear hijack my life forever. I created a fear bigger than life itself and convinced myself if I came out, it would kill my mom, due to her present medical conditions. I knew my dad's health was also not good and I didn't want to burden them.

But these were all 'stories' that I created to stop myself from being me – to stop myself from living the life that I wanted. Finally knowing that the dream that I had before wasn't mine, but of the people around me. I realized that I already lost 9 years of my life struggling to hide who I am, and trying to live a dream that was far from what I wanted. Now I can happily say I have gotten my life back, my family back, and I am now committed to living the way I was always meant to; free spirited and passionately.

~ *T. Hossain* ~

Photo: Wack N'gouna, Senegal, by Nilmi Senaratna

My entire life I believed I had an amazing destiny. I was going to be someone special, assist people and change lives. Yet, after years of depression, dysfunctional relationships, welfare, being diagnosed with bi-polar, personality and pre-menstrual dysphoric disorder, and experiencing the woes of many, many failed dreams, I was ready to give up. For a while I told myself all the pain and suffering would be for a good cause. The dark tunnel would end and then there would be light. But time passed and nothing changed. Instead, my hopeful attitude diminished leaving me face to face with grief and dismay. I sunk deeper and deeper; becoming dangerous not only to myself but to those nearest and dearest to me. I convinced myself that I deserved all these 'bad' experiences, not realizing it was I, and my mindset, that was creating them. I led myself to believe that this was my life, so much so that I was willing to hold onto this belief, even if it killed me! That is until recently...

After another failed relationship with someone I deeply loved, I decided I needed to take some time for myself and travel. Though on the brink of bankruptcy, I needed to get away and do something for myself. I planned to explore four countries in three months, and give myself the space to recalibrate.

I'm not exactly sure what it was but as I traversed through these foreign lands, my mind started to shift. I met some amazing people who opened my eyes to new perspectives and possibilities I never considered. The tools they shared, and how they had benefitted them in their life, suddenly made me realize that the destiny I had always dreamed of having was available and right there in front of me. I, however, couldn't see it because my life was clouded with all the pain and sadness I was choosing to hang onto.

These new friends, who I consider angels, introduced me to meditation, books and ideas which allowed me to begin the process of releasing all the garbage that was clogging my mind. I realized I needed to leave the crap behind and focus on what it was I wanted in my life now. While many things came to mind, the main desires included having love and happiness in my life.

The amazing thing about life is when you open yourself up, accept that people are coming into your life for a particular reason and see experiences as valuable life lessons, 'stuff' instantly starts to happen! As the days passed and I began to let go, a whole new world was revealed. I saw that the world WAS filled with an abundance of opportunities. I was simply choosing to live in a very small limiting space because I thought if it wasn't available in my past, then it wasn't available in my future.

I realized that every experience, the failed relationships and traumas, were not hardwired to my being. I recognize that I had to have these experiences, so that I could go to these places, meet these angels and discover a new level of understanding. The ideal life that I sought was very real and available.

After my trip, I returned to Australia and realized my journey is just in its infancy. While I am still learning, the most important thing was to be mindful of my thoughts. Though the thoughts of my past relationships, financial burdens and diagnosis' still come to mind, thanks to meditation and other tools I have begun to practice, I am able to acknowledge them without dwelling on them. This allows me to then step into a world of true peace and joy.

I am now in a place where I boastfully exude how far I've come! I see my experiences as reminders for where I've been and a place where I don't want to be ever again. I realize that I can have or be anything, and that I deserve love and happiness. But deserving it doesn't bring it to fruition; nor does more medication and therapy. It is I who has to be loving and happy, and THAT comes with letting go and not holding onto the pain from my past.

Because I no longer live in a limiting space, I have some ballsy things planned for my future. Although I don't have all the answers, I know that if I believe in myself, practice mindfulness and continue to let go, my dream destiny will happen.

~ *Yvonne Scully* ~

Passion over Past

Sexually harassed and molested by people I least expected made growing up in Morocco a peculiar situation. Of the Africa, Arab and Muslim worlds, Moroccan women have leaped forward, and I am well aware of these advances. But there are still no laws that protect women against harassment, so I learned to defend myself; how to stand on my own and assert myself in a male dominant society.

I grew up in a sheltered family environment. I studied in the beautifully gardened French missionary school in a lovely neighborhood where I knew everyone. We all came from educated families and respected each other. We hardly ever saw the miners and less fortunate people – we were very innocent girls and boys. We all played sports and did activities together. I never felt I was looked at sexually or in any physically suggestive way.

After I received my high school diploma, I went to Casablanca to pursue my university education. This is when my sheltered life was shattered. There, sexual harassment incidents were a daily occurrence. Walking the streets and taking the bus were very hazardous activities. In the streets, men walked beside and behind me with lusting eyes. They would start with nice comments and compliments, and request that I stop to have a coffee or tea. When I did not respond, the verbal abuse would begin and that's when my heart would start pounding. I had to learn tactics to keep the men away. One thing I did was walk closely to an older man or woman who had a child. Only then would they 'back off.' The verbal harassment would last anywhere between five minutes to an hour – however long it took for me to get to my destination safely. Sometimes I would stop in a store to buy something; hoping that the abuser would go. Sometimes this worked, but other times it did not. Then I would request help from the shop owner or a costumer and beg them to accompany me to the university. Riding the bus was an adventure as well. Overcrowded buses allowed men to rub up against you. My survival techniques here included locating an empty spot where my back would be resting on the sides or windows of the bus, and put my school bag in front of me as a shield. Or I would find a group of girls and stand beside them. I had to not only worry about pick pocketing thieves, but perverts as well. Once a lady on the bus was in her traditional Moroccan djellabas. A man came behind her and started to masturbate. He then ejaculated on her – soiling the back of her dress. I can still vividly remember this experience.

Three months after I started university, I was waiting at the bus stop to go back to the campus dormitory. I was dressed modestly in blue jeans, a wind breaker, hair braided, a backpack, and no make-up. I remember it so clearly: a man, about 65 years old, pulled to the side of the road with his black shiny Mercedes. It was 5pm; I was alone at the bus stop, but it was still light outside. The man lowered his window and asked me to get in his car. I did not know what to do. He started to offer me rates for sexual acts: he would give me this much money for doing this or that. I panicked; my heart beat was deafening my ears. I started to walk backwards and looked in all directions, and then the verbal abuse and profanities started. Suddenly out of nowhere, a soldier came forward from under a tree. The man rolled his window up and left. The soldier looked at me and asked which bus I was waiting for; he then requested that I stay close to him. I phoned my parents once I got to my room and in between tears I told them about the incident. They decided to buy me a Vespa, which would be my new mode of transportation. I was so grateful for this Vespa; I feel it drastically reduced my incidences of sexual harassment.

I could attribute all these incidences during my first three months to ignorance, resentment, lack of education, sexual suppression by socio-cultural customs and other things. But nothing had prepared me for what was to come. It was my senior year in 1995 and I was sure of two things: I wanted to continue my postgraduate education, and I was open to all possibilities of education in Morocco and abroad. I applied to higher institutes in Morocco; as well, I was preparing applications to universities in the UK, USA and Canada. For the international applications, I asked my professors for advice and help and sought a letter of reference from one of my professors, because he had studied in America. He introduced me to another man, André, whom I continue to hold in high regard, who was visiting from America. He was offering an assistantship in America for MA students who majored in English and spoke French very well. After we met in a café, exchanged words in French and got to know each other, André was impressed with my capabilities. The meeting ended with him promising to send the application for the assistantship as soon as he got back to America. As a thank you, my parents invited my professor to dinner in one of the most exclusive clubs in Casablanca.

The fact that my professor met my family, shared a meal with them (a sacred act in Moroccan culture), and had an American wife along with a child, left me no reason to not trust him. Once I received the application from André, I contacted my professor who requested that we meet at the American Cultural Center. He explained that I had everything for the application; I only needed to prepare a statement. I had never done this, so he offered to help. Computers were rare in Morocco in 1995, but my professor had one at his home, so he invited me to go with him to his house to work on the statement. I agreed without any hesitation because in my mind his wife would be there. Once we got to his place, I noticed the house was empty. He explained that his wife was in America. My mind was racing but I thought that he is an honorable man, a professor, plus he met my family, so all was fine. For 2 hours we worked on the statement on his computer. When we finished, he printed the statement and I was ready to leave but that's when he asked me to wait a minute. He went inside one of the rooms, I thought he went to the bathroom, and returned wearing a bathrobe. Then he opened it – he was completely naked. As I write this, I feel the same fear gripping my body. I had no idea what to do. He started asking me all kinds of very personal questions. I told him that I was a virgin and that I never engaged in any intercourse. He started to caress me but I stood there frozen; frigid with fear and disgust. I did not move from my chair. I clasped my hands around my body and said nothing. After thirty minutes of him caressing me, he pushed me hard and left. I assume he went to masturbate because after some time I heard the shower. I took my documents and left.

The next day I sent my application to André at Illinois State University. I was admitted to ISU and started my MA in June 1996. I told my parents about the incident and my dad called my professor two days later. Although he did not mention anything about the incident, he thanked him for his help. He then said, "Samira is like your daughter or your younger sister, and we thank you very much for being such a noble and caring professor." My dad's message was more degrading than thankful and I hope that he felt the magnitude of what he did.

About three months later, André called me and asked to explain if something was wrong with his friend. Apparently, my professor had contacted him and mentioned that I may not be a good choice for an assistantship and that he should drop my file and he would recommend another student. I explained what happened to André who completely understood, and never acted on the suggestion.

That phone call from André was very important. It was the moment when I realized my vulnerability and my power. I stood up, as much as I could, to a sexual predator/pervert. More than ever in life, I knew then that I needed to pursue and excel at my education. I went to America armed with a resolute sense of who I was, how to protect myself, how to defend myself, and how to ensure that I have the power to break the circle. Now when I visit Morocco and I am harassed in the street, I stop and stand up to those who verbally abuse me. They run away because the confidence emanating from me overshadows their lust. This incident with my professor left me with a sense of disgust and disappointment towards someone who practices in a noble profession. Even though this type of behavior can be found anywhere, the main problem I had to overcome was the fact that there was nothing in the university handbook that protects victims with these issues. I could not go to an office in the university and complain. There was no system in place. If I have to think about it, feminism started to root in me at that moment. This is when I started to think about building support networks for women dealing with a variety of harassment issues. Baby steps have been taken regarding rape and sexual harassment in Morocco. Although much more needs to be done, we continue into the 21st century with hope that some seeds for change have been planted.

~ Samira ElAtia ~

"Say thank you, no matter how small the favor or insignificant the gesture."

~ Daria Brown ~

AT 13 years of age a neighbor sexually abused me. This was probably the most difficult time of my life, and all my hopes and dreams seemed to just fade away. I was emotionally consumed by this experience; confused and alone. I couldn't focus on any of my future dreams and lost my appetite of life. I even wanted to stop going to school, because I thought there is no use of it in my life now. Sometimes I would sit alone, ashamed and ask myself, "Why did this happen to me? Why not to another person instead?" It was all I could think about.

Most days in class, if the teacher was asking a question, even if I knew the answer, I could not raise my hand, because I was afraid what people might say. Yet no one knew my secret, and I continued living with these horrible feelings.

More than a year had passed, then one Saturday afternoon while at home, alone, as everyone was out, going about their business, and I had nothing to do…I said to myself, "Ok, today is the day to do something different." But what will that something be? Because up to this point, every time I tried to do anything, all I could think about was, "I'm not sure if I can do this." Then I would end up doing nothing at all again. But this day was different, there was an adult meeting in my Church, and I thought, I could just pop in for a couple of minutes.

The pastor started teaching, making his usual points and perspectives, but today a few words he spoke would change my life forever. He said we are very important people; we are all strong and can make a difference in our society. He continued with, that we are here for 'a special purpose', not by accident. This stuck with me... 'A special purpose'. These simple words were a turning point. I could focus on a future again, because I was important. This day, I was happy that I went to church.

Soon I started feeling better. My dreams of becoming someone, someone special, started to come back to life. I was transforming, and I began telling myself what had happened was now in my past, and I have a race to run, a journey to make a difference. This past experience does not define me. I decided to continue with my studies, focus on my dreams, and choose to feel alive again. Now I'm happy and running a race to my destiny, making a difference in my life and society.

~ Pina ~

Photo: *The Blue City in Jodhpur, India by Elisa De Pascali*

Having been called many things over the years – Mixed, Black, Brown, Spanish, Mulato, Oreo, Brownie…these words have never offended me, because having a Canadian Mom and a Trinidadian Dad I guess I just got used to it. When I was younger, I can recall at least two or three times where people would ask my Mom if I was adopted. Growing up with these naive comments became the norm. I didn't really believe that they were racist, just curious. However, there was the one time that no words were said, but a loud message was conveyed, and I was truly hurt.

While visiting my aunt and cousins in Manitoba, we all went to play mini golf. It was a great game, and I got two holes in one! When the game was over, I raced back to the clubhouse because they had a sign that said anyone with a hole in one got a free surprise. I got there before everyone else and was yelling, "I got a hole in one! I got a hole in one!" and as I said that I reached into the basket to pick out my prize. One of the workers came out, took one look at me and scowled saying, "Get your hands out of there, you didn't get a hole in one" and yanked the basket away. As he was doing this my mom came in and said, "Yes she did, now give the basket back." Afterward, as we sat and enjoyed ice cream the attendant kept glaring at me. Other families came and went, took their hole in one prizes and nothing was said. This is where the pieces started coming together… The only difference I could see was that I didn't look like the other kids. Later we walked out to the parking lot and while we stood talking, I heard a noise, looked up and saw the golf attendant putting garbage in the dumpster. I watched him wondering why he was so mean. As he walked back towards the clubhouse, he stopped, looked directly at me, and spit on the ground. I was utterly shocked and told my aunt and mom about it later.

It was hard to believe that someone who didn't know me could dislike me so much. I considered the situation for hours, wondering what I had done. Maybe if I had asked to take something from the bucket that wouldn't have happened, but the hatred coming from this man was difficult to take. It made me question who I was. Maybe he was right, maybe my existence was an insult, maybe I was just no good.

After the mini-golf experience, writing has proven to be very therapeutic. I wrote out how I was feeling, my perception of what happened, and drew a picture. Over the years, writing short stories became a passion and also a healing process. Whenever a difficult situation comes up, I write about it. It helps me lay everything out, to be completely honest with myself, and allows me the space to first vent, then to reflect and learn the lesson that comes from every struggle. Even if the words flowing out don't seem logical, I've learned to trust the process and to allow myself time and space.

The experience I had when I was 12 really made me question my self-worth. But writing about it was the first step toward healing and transforming that experience. Because of this I now believe it is beneficial to regularly take an objective look at my life. I take a step back and look for all the things I am grateful for; the beauty around me, what I have accomplished, the important people in my life, and the impact I have on them. For me it is a way of seeing my self-worth and my inherent nature.

Objective tallies can help pull you out of uncertainty. If it works for you, write; write until your hand goes numb. Get everything out of your head and onto paper so you can be free. Writing continues to help me and maybe, just maybe, it will have the same impact on you.

~ Katelyn Butler-Birmingham ~

It started as a tingling

In my hands then feet
I'd shake them to wake them
As I'd walk down the street

Then came the ringing
Hurting my ears
High in pitch
That no-one else could hear

I went to a doctor
Nothing was wrong
I dismissed it all
I kept moving on

I was busy
Selling houses
On top of my game
14 hours a day
7 days a week
It was all the same

E-mails and texts
Appointments and calls
It got so big
I couldn't do it all

I hired an assistant
I hired two
The more I worked
The more it grew

I got so tired
I could not sleep
The buzzing in my ears
The tingling - now pain
In my hands and feet

20 more years
Ensued
20 more years
The symptoms grew
20 more doctors
20 more healers
More treatments
More tests
MRI's, cat scans
And alternative things
More symptoms
More questions
Few answers
No Clues

There's nothing wrong
That we're worried about

It's all in your head
They said
Take a year off
Go to bed
Rest
You're stressed
Take these meds

Bullshit I said!
The only THING that's in my head
Is an electrical shock
Every minute or two
The ringing in my ears
Won't disappear
The left side of my body
Goes completely numb
I collapse to the floor every now and then
And stutter and slur for an hour or two
I've got constant pain
In my hands, limbs and feet
I cannot sleep
I've got chronic fatigue
9 weeks of diarrhoea
And vomiting

I'm so dehydrated
I need intravenous drips
I'm dizzy as hell from the vertigo

I'm nauseous, I can't eat
I can't concentrate
I can't remember things
My writings all inverted
Like dyslexia
I'm severely depressed
I've got pressure in my chest
Sleep apnoea
And shortness of breath
Thyroiditis
Abdominal and ovarian pain
Floaters in my eyes
Sharp pains in my teeth
Skin rashes, burning and itching
Has got me beat

It's not in my head
I said!
If this is my life
I'd rather be dead!

Suddenly my doctor
Surprise in his eyes
Looked up at me
You know, I think you may have
This new thing…
This…
Electro-Hyper-Sensitivity

I've just learned about this
He apologized
I'm sorry, there's little I can do
I've actually never seen someone like you
But there's a clinic I can refer you to

When I checked it out
I had 60 symptoms of the 72

I dropped my career
Of 24 years
The life I knew

I ran
To a small depressed beach town
It was winter then
Deserted, dismal and blue
But my mom lived there
And I needed her
To wrap my arms around
And talk to

I bought a house up the street
Walking distance to the beach
I fixed it up for my
Electric, magnetic
And hard-wired needs

8 months went by
I felt better by then
As long as I didn't stray
From the beach, my house
And the walks in between
And stayed away
From people with cells,
Electric, magnetic and wireless things

We spent many a night
My mom and me
In safety
Away from the world I knew
Playing scrabble
Eating healthy foods
And cheating on ice cream
Laughing, talking and dreaming
Of the things we wanted to do
Walking to the beach and back again
Wrapping arms around and loving my best friend

Then one day, suddenly
My mom was taken to emergency
They opened her up
She was bleeding inside
And 2 days later, she had died

Oh how I cried
The unbearable ache inside

Then one day
I stumbled upon a light
I followed it
I meditated
I prayed morning noon and night
God help me please
I don't know what to do
I'm so lonely, I'm so scared
I'm so through
With being terrified
To go out in this world
I don't want to survive
I want to thrive
Please, please
I'm down on my knees
Oh God help me
Please, please!

CHANGE!

What?

CHANGE!

But it's not me,
It's…

CHANGE!

What - Change me?

And then,
More gently
Softly
The voice replied
Change what you see
Change what you feel
Nothing need be real
But what you make it to be

I was stunned
Alarmed
Excited
Aghast with disbelief
Holy shi…
Gosh!
God's talking to me!
                     ~ Lucy Sanford ~

Riding the Go Train to Aldershot Station every single weeknight – leaving behind the stresses of working in Toronto's concrete jungle. Unwinding from a tiresome day was always the same on the train; find the coziest seat by the window, set an alarm on my BlackBerry, smush my coat into a makeshift pillow and insert ear plugs to drown out the noise. Fifty minutes flies by when I sleep deep. It was time to get up. I stretched out into my human form, instead of the contorted hamster I looked like when I slept and that's when I felt the pain. At first, I thought it was just a kink from my nap, but the pain persisted. Slowly I trudged to my car – tired, struggling to keep my eyes open and still with thirty minutes left before I got home. I wasn't exactly energetic for a 25 year old, so I decided to skip dinner, cancel my social plans and head straight to bed. My parents asked if I was okay and mentioned that I've been sleeping a lot lately. I muttered that I might be coming down with a cold so sleep should boost my immune system. The side pain had diminished, but I still felt my shoulder aching, so I took some painkillers and went to bed.

That night I dreamt in black and white (not my usual technicolor). As I was standing in the middle of the sidewalk, strangers passed me by as if I didn't exist. I noticed that no one spoke – some people wore hospital gowns and every single one was expressionless. Near the end of the dream, I turned my head and came face to face with myself. I looked at my doppelgänger and waited to see what would happen next. Of course, right before I woke up the doppelgänger said, "Go to the hospital." After those words were spoken in my dream I woke up gasping for breath. It felt like a jagged knife was repeatedly stabbing me under my rib. I noticed that my shoulder felt worse; like it was on fire! This was not good. I glanced at the cellphone beside my head and realized it was 1:53am. There wasn't a doubt in my mind what I had to do next. I struggled to get up since each breath caused more pain and less oxygen. Now I understood what shortness of breath meant. I snuck out of the house in my pajamas to avoid any unnecessary worry for my parents (just in case it was nothing) and drove to the nearest emergency room. Hours went by, and the excruciating pain continued, even the painkillers I was given wore off quickly. Finally, a doctor came and said a blood sample was needed to test my INR (International Normalized Ratio) level. This test determined how thick or thin my blood was. He looked at me seriously and said, "It's to check if you have blood clots. If the levels aren't normal you'll be sent up for a CAT scan." I didn't panic because I had no idea what having a blood clot meant. I called home and my dad came to the hospital. I told him they were doing some precautionary tests and not to worry. The test came back an hour later and I was wheeled up for the first CAT scan in my life. My father had arrived by that point and was told to wait in the emergency waiting room for my return. The scan itself wasn't scary; in fact, I was so delirious that I told the technician the machine looked like a doughnut and that I was the jelly going inside. A sense of humor in serious situations has always been my first coping mechanism and it didn't fail me there. As I was wheeled back to the emergency room a nurse said the doctor would be back with the results in thirty minutes and she went to get my dad. My heart broke looking at my father's face when the doctor approached us and said, "You are one lucky lady. I have no idea how you are still alive. We found multiple blood clots in your lower right lung. Someone must be watching out for you." At that moment a hundred thoughts flooded my mind. *Do I need surgery? How do we break these clots? Are they damaging me right now? Will I lose a lung? How long will I feel pain each time I breathe? I can't miss work. Why does dad look so sad? I can't miss work. Do I need to take medication? We have to call mom. What am I going to do about work?* The magnitude of my situation didn't resonate with me until I familiarized myself with what a pulmonary embolism was. Statistically people who have pulmonary embolisms usually never find out because they drop dead.

I was in awe. For some reason, God performed a miracle for me and I was given a second chance at life. People say that it takes a near death experience to change a person's life and that was true for me.

It took about 1 year of visits with doctors, specialists, and finally taking a DNA test to uncover I had a genetic blood disorder. The medical professionals call it Factor V Leiden. While nearly every aspect of my life was altered or impacted on September 30th, 2011, I believe God has a destiny for everyone and the events in my life were meant to be. Not everyone will see the reason for what He does in our lives but I think if you just let go and believe in his awesomeness, it will be revealed to you in the most unique ways. I always loved the poem *Footprints* by Mary Stevenson as a child and found it to be filled with such powerful words. Many times in life I have thought I was alone. However, that event showed me that God has always been there carrying me when I needed His help. This wasn't the first time He intervened and I believe it won't be the last.

This transformation left me with a new sense of empowerment over my life. Within the first month of being home on bed rest I had a lot of time to think. I realized that the times I was stressed out or somehow sucked into someone else's problems was because I allowed myself to be a part of that situation. I allowed myself to feel the stress and allowed others to suck my positive energy dry. From then on I decided I would never allow other people's emotions, problems, or self-created dramas to negatively influence my own life ever again. Interestingly, I had this mantra within me all this time but sometimes it takes an intense situation for a person to realize what they need to do in their life to live a true happy life! My newly uncovered mantra affected every aspect of my life and it felt like the hope of an amazing 'new' life was pumping through my veins. The realization that I was not invincible, nor do I know when my death is supposed to come, is what truly made me think what do I want to contribute to this world? I wanted to Pay it Forward and become the most passionate global citizen I could be; be that through telling my story, doing random acts of kindness, listening to a stranger, volunteering my time to a charity or spending more time with my loved ones.

Whatever it was, I knew that my life would forever be changed. It's not an easy journey by any means, but I always have the reminder of why I don't need to stress the small things. There are more important things in life than making a lot of money, and when I am down the only way back, is UP. Talking about this event in my life can never do it justice because each person experiences things differently. The sheer inspiration and 'aha' I developed was incredible and the one thing I want people to know from my experience is that finding passion can change your life. A reason that makes you smile and happy each day, one that gives you the power to take risks, have no regrets and take every experience as a step towards your ultimate path.

~ Magdalena H Brzoska ~

At 8 years old I had nail marks up my arms, a bruised eye and torn panties. My innocence couldn't make sense that a senior student had just tried to rape me. I went home, not sure what had just happened. I didn't even know if anything *had* happend – it was just a regular day at school. The instant my mother became aware of the situation, she interrogated me asking, "What happened?! What did *he* do?" After hours of questions, no action was taken and the 'incident' was brushed under the rug. Not surprising, as the Pakistani community would have shunned our family. After all, Pakistani women don't get raped, so how could a little girl?! Pakistani women had to be submissive to men, and in the event that something *did* occur, no one would believe it. The woman would be accused of making it up. I know my parents worried what their friends would think if anyone found out. How could they ever find their daughter a suitor when it came time for marriage if this got out?

I am 22 now and to this day the issue about 'what happened' that day has never been discussed. At one point in high school, I did mention it to my mother since at the time I was struggling to build trusting relationships. She told me I was crazy and a 'good' mother like her would never let something like that happen. But what she fails to understand is she wasn't there when *it* happened.

My life continued – I couldn't maintain friendships or hug people. Talking to men, in spite of culture restrictions, was awkward and often led to panic attacks. My mother became very controlling after the 'incident'. Not only did she restrict me from going out with people, she wouldn't let me call or speak to anyone unless she could listen to the conversation on the other end.

My family was poor; after all, there were 8 of us, so I had to get a job to support myself at a young age. At 13 years old I became the take-out girl at a local restaurant, and I did a good enough job that the manager allowed me to hire people from school, and train them in their roles. This is when I met Jenna. She was very charming and charismatic – a people pleaser (like me), and eager to start her first job. At first I was a little alarmed that at 22 this was her first job, but I didn't pay much attention to it. As time went on, we became closer. I wanted to hang out with Jenna, but my mother never allowed it. I was 15 now and one day when I asked my mother if I could hang out, for whatever reason she said 'ok'. I was allowed to go to the mall with Jenna on the condition that she would be there shopping for her personal things. Eventually, my mother loved Jenna. Jenna had a certain allure to her that won my mother over. This was good, but I still had many restrictions. A day came when I was simply fed up with my mother and her restrictions, and we had a horrible argument. I wasn't allowed to go to parties, I wasn't even allowed to attend sex or drug education classes at school. I was a good kid, why could she not accept it and let me go out with people so I could build confidence and character? I was so upset with her restrictions on me that I saw this as an opportunity to do something and give her a reason to be upset with me. So during school lunchtime one day, my friends and I went to get our belly buttons pierced. It was perhaps the most painful moment of my life, but I did it!

After school I panicked; I didn't want to go home. I was bleeding profusely, so I decided to go to work until the bleeding was controlled. My managers found out what I did because I bled straight through my shirt. They helped me bandage the area. After leaving work, Jenna met up with me and while we walked, I raged with anger about my mother. Just then Jenna offered me a cigarette. I had never tried smoking or done anything like this before, but Jenna said, "Go big or go home. Do all the crazy shit now, so your mother gets mad at you only once. This way you've lived!" So, I grabbed the cigarette and took a puff. After the first puff, I was dizzy and my mouth was dry, so Jenna gave me a bottle of juice to drink. It turned out the juice had three, triple stacked tablets of ecstasy mixed into it and it was a bad batch. Without knowing, I overdosed and began hallucinating. Before this, I had absolutely no idea what drugs were, not even weed. This was because of the lack of education I got thanks to my mother's restrictions and our cultural restrictions.

I later found out the reason why Jenna never held a job until she was 22 was because she was diagnosed with schizophrenia, bipolar and various personality disorders. This wasn't the first time she attempted to harm someone; it was habit. Until my case, none of her past victims had ever come forward so she carried on as a normal citizen. My brain had 2 holes in it from the drugs I took. I suffered from short-term memory loss, and to this day I still struggle with my memory. Once everyone at school found out what happened, I became the outcast. Everything I had so desperately worked for was gone. Even my manager at the restaurant kindly asked me to resign, so he didn't have to fire me. Although my mother was devastated by what happened, this incident was good for her too. After the incident, she stopped caring what people in our community thought of her and our family; she just wanted us to follow our dreams and passions. After this incident I started to get support from her.

I ended up graduating high school a year early. I had the highest marks in my class, but no friends. I felt like an empty body alone and forgotten. Although I was off to university with a dream to become the best corporate lawyer and a goal to be the best person I could possibly be, I became depressed with PTSD (Post-Traumatic Stress Disorder) and suffered from anxiety.

At one point during the semester, one of my Professors was arranging an event and I was picked as one of the top three students to attend. I learned that Yale, an Ivy League School, was seeking five transfer students; individuals who would like to change the world and weren't afraid of adversity, challenges and failure. I passed the entry test and my Professor wrote me a recommendation letter stating the Canadian Ivy League School I was attending was not challenging enough for me. Ultimately with his blessing, and out of hundreds of students, I was chosen to participate. The next day I had a 100 hour case study to do. I got only 8 hours sleep in four days, but I completed the work. Although those four days were hell, I got through it, and a week later I was given an offer letter for admission.

I think the important takeaway here is that life just has a way of working out. Everyone goes through a unique experience and faces many challenges, but your passions are what make you stand out from the crowd and are your fuel to success! Passion is unique to everyone, and it challenges you against adversity. I have faced a lot in my short life; rape, drugs, and eating disorders, but now I'm off to an Ivy League institution. All of this was only possible because I never thought about failure as regret – it was simply a wakeup call for me to think and act differently. After meeting Laska Paré at work one day, I changed for good. Laska added happiness, hope and confidence to my life. Just looking at her exuberant character, contagious sense of kindness, and loving spirit of life makes you truly understand that anything is possible! It also presents you with a moment of reflection of how important it is to be kind to everyone you meet, because you don't know anyone's battles, and you have absolutely no idea how you may impact their life.

What has happened in my life has only made me stronger and now that I look back, I'm happy with the strength and courage I've gathered from my experiences. My passion for wanting to help others, and being really good at what I do, have propelled me towards a happier life. Remember, that fire in you is something you should always give in to because it will take you to wonderful places!

Now, as I look onwards to the future, it's even more clear that even though I may still have challenging experiences, every day adds to my next moment. Right now is a moment of discovery, and our past is simply a teacher. I hope that everyone who reads this can understand that life only gets better and better. Just do what you love, stay focused and always remain positive. The best things in life are free, but sometimes they take time to obtain. Your passions will outweigh your past, always.

~ Jasmine ~

Photo: Nugegoda, Sri Lanka, by Nilmi Senaratna

During a personal development course I was attending, the women and men were separated. Once the men left the room, the teacher indicated we would be partaking in a playful dance exercise. Our task was to be feminine with one another through dance and movement. We were instructed to feel our femininity and playfulness as we danced around and enjoyed each other's energies. Once the exercise began, all the women flowed around the room dancing sensually and playfully, laughing and smiling. Yet, I stood there awkwardly. I felt uncomfortable and shy as if I didn't belong with these free feminine spirits. I tried to mimic the motions and dance moves of the women but I slowly felt myself becoming paralyzed, and the feeling was getting stronger. It came to a point where eventually I just stood on the side lines while all the women danced their sexy bodies in motion. When the teacher noticed my paralyzed state, she came over and asked if I was ok. I told her the emotions I was experiencing and she indicated there might have been something in my past that was causing these feelings. After the exercise was complete, everyone openly discussed what they experienced during the exercise. As my turn approached, I felt myself getting nervous. I was uncomfortable and on edge, but I reminded myself I was in a safe space. As I shared my experience, tears began to fill my eyes but I had no idea why. Feeling ashamed and vulnerable, the teacher asked if I would consider writing about the first time I ever felt feminine. I agreed, so here goes...

I was about 7 or 8 years old when I put on my new pink snow suit. It was a snowy winter day and my pink snowsuit made me feel like such a girl, but not just any girl, a cute feminine girl! Though the snow suit was big and thick, it fit me like a glove and made me feel sexy. This is the first time I had felt this way about myself.

Once suited up, a friend and I headed to the park to go tobogganing. On top of this hilly area, we came upon some boys who were also tobogganing. We joined them and one of the little boys became very fond of me. He asked if he could go down the hill with me and my toboggan, to which I agreed and he hoped on. He hugged me tight from behind as we excitedly went fast down the hill. When we reached the bottom of the hill we were alone as everyone was still at the top. Then this little boy started humping me vigorously. I was shocked, startled and confused – not understanding what was happening. I feel in this moment I told myself a 'story' to explain the situation – that it was not safe to feel sexy; that being a girl and feeling sexy or sensual makes you vulnerable and creates an opportunity to be taken advantage of. Looking back, I can now see how this experience, and my understanding of it, affected me, and has ruled parts of my life since. After this, I became very masculine in character; I liked riding motorcycles like my dad, being handy with his tools, and then purchased my first home on my own. These traits made me believe, "I don't really need a man around." When it came to dating, I much preferred the sensitive men over the macho manly guys; that way, I would be in control and could dominate the relationship.

I realize now, after working in the beauty industry for many years as a color technician, that the passionate way I have been expressing my femininity was by making my clients beautiful and making them feel feminine. Understanding this now and although on the outside I look like an attractive woman (lipstick, heels and all), and I love my work, I've chosen to bring back my feminine, sexy side and feel fully myself again, renewed.

By releasing this 'story' about this experience, and the 7-year-old self I created, I now have access to who I truly am. I am a sensual, sexy and feminine being who loves to play! I am free to express who I am. Feeling beautiful inside and out, and being comfortable with my femininity is truly blissful. And although my masculine side will always be a part of who I am, I am no longer repressing my female energy. I am a woman; powerful, and free to always be me – passionately.

~ Charlene Guzzo ~

How I spent 15 years of my life trapped in the sex trade – not knowing if I'd get out or if I'd even survive, I don't know. Men beat me, raped me and I became a serious drug addict. I would yell at God all the time. I could hear his whispers but they fell on deaf ears.

My parents were involved in the church when I was a little girl and Jesus was my imaginary friend. At only 5 years old my brother's friend sexually abused me every week, over a 3 year period. When my parents split up I was happy because it meant the family would move and the weekly torment would end, but it also meant my dad was no longer in my life. At age 9, I was raped again.

At 12 years of age I started drinking, doing drugs and having sex. I then met an 18-year-old boy and we began dating, but he was violent. One time he threw a screwdriver that stuck in my head. At 14 I ended up pregnant – I was happy and excited, thinking this baby girl would finally give me the love I so craved. But I soon realized I was not ready for a baby and gave the child to my mom. I asked my minister to baptize my daughter and he refused because she was 'born out of sin'. After that, I decided to have nothing to do with God again. I was having sex with all kinds of men, feeling lost without my father around, as my parents were now divorced, and my very broken family was based on a lot of lies. I was always angry.

My road to destruction continued when at only 17 I married a violent man who was in and out of jail. While he was in jail he sent his friend Bill to keep an eye on me. Bill seemed kind and was nice to me, and the children (by now I'd had another child). Meanwhile, my husband was put into a halfway house from prison and repeatedly threatened me, until one evening he came to my mom's house and the police were called. The next morning, Bill arrived on my doorstep and assured me not to worry. We left the kids with my mom and went for a drive, while Bill explained that all is fine now, as he had killed my husband and I was going to help bury him. Fearful now for my life, I helped to get rid of the evidence and then remained a captive sex slave for the next three years. After being repeatedly raped and tortured I eventually found the nerve to call the police. Bill got a life sentence and I did my time doing community service.

At 21, I started working in a massage parlor and prostitution followed through my twenties and thirties. This led to drinking heavily, doing drugs and cutting myself to ease the pain and to dull my shame. And now I had two more children, fathered by my pimp. Now my firstborn daughter had become a Christian at age 12, and would leave Bible scriptures on my door and drag me to church with her. I hated it and didn't believe God cared at all. I ended up finally getting out of the business only because I fell for one of my customers. He promised to take care of my kids and me. He did take care of me but I soon became his personal sex slave. He ended up leaving me three years later.

I was mentally a mess – a drug addict – and fell into deep depression. When my husband left me I was left with nothing. I had no money to move and I pondered going back to the business. Through my daughter I met a couple who eventually became my mentors and they generously gave me first and last months rent. After realizing if I went back to prostitution I would die, I took these people up on their offer and then felt obligated to go to church. I started to attend and hated it. They were offering an Alpha course and Sheila, the woman who gave me the money, said she would go if I did. I again felt obligated and went. I trusted no one and really just went to please her. It was the ninth week in and I had asked all the questions I think you could possibly ask in this course, as I had no filter. I still did not believe in God and was there only to please Sheila. But the dinners were awesome! That night I came to the course really broken, they had separated into small groups to pray, but I didn't want to be a part of it, so I sat at the table with Sheila. I left crying uncontrollably and drove around crying. I pulled over and sat in silence until I heard someone say, "You have tried everything else just give me a try, what have you got to lose?" I knew that voice and I thought, "You are right." I asked God to help me forgive myself and although there were no fireworks, in that moment I felt a peace that I had never experienced before. I realized then that God was real and he was with me.

Since then Sheila and her husband, Todd, became my spiritual parents. I always felt like I had something inside me that wasn't good. I would hear voices in my head all the time. I think when you go through sexual abuse or any kind of trauma that you become emotionally disoriented. During a prayer session I blanked out – thrashed about and apparently was telling them that the devil was in me, but they just kept on praying. When I awoke I realized I no longer heard the voices. The next day was the first time at church I could hear the pastor's message without the voices. A miracle had happened.

With this second chance I decided to give back to my community and now I speak in schools, to the police and at Defend Dignity conferences and other events across the country. I now have a passion to fight against human trafficking, and my church has made me an urban missionary. I am now an active voice in fighting for women and against prostitution. I have my own organization called *Rising Angels*, that helps woman get out of this darkness. I still struggle, but for the first time I am not alone, nor am I angry. I do have post traumatic stress, but I can deal with it because I have love in my life and I have God. Passion and my community have helped me overcome my past.

Last Fall I was married, although two years ago I tattooed my ring finger with the Alpha-Omega symbol because I truly believed I would never get married. It's funny that my dreams of marriage as a little girl have been answered. I believe God answers our prayers when we are ready.

~ Katarina MacLeod ~

"*An unwavering quiet wraps around your shoulders;
a silence that settles there as you search for the words.
Words that will mend the part that is broken,
whispered on the wind as you pass by.
If you allow the silence to embrace you,
and the words to speak to you,
you will find that, maybe…
You have already been healed.*"

~ April McIntyre ~

Every human wants to feel a sense of belonging and acceptance from other people. Looking back at my relatively short life of 30 years, I have struggled with this need for belonging and acceptance for most of it because of my sexual orientation.

I was born and raised in Toronto by a very conservative, Korean immigrant family. Along with being brought up in a right-wing Christian community, and with expectations about 'what kind of man I was going to marry' and 'by what age this significant event was going to happen' was something discussed regularly at dinners with family, relatives and other church friends. This marriage conversation became more frequent as I was entering my late teens, and I used to go along with these conversations without much contemplation as getting married was something that seemed like it was going to happen so far away in the future, if ever at all. But as I reached my early twenties, I knew that these marriage conversations were no longer something I could easily brush off anymore. By then, I was certain that the possibility of me getting married to a man, as everyone around me had frequently expressed, was very slim since the people I had become attracted to for the last several years had been mostly women.

Expectations, in general, are really horrible to put on people as it sets them up for failure; however, having expectations on people based on a set of assumptions you have about who they are as a human being is a whole other layer of awfulness to deal with. And so when I started to discover during my preteens that my sexual orientation was not that of the mainstream, I chose to conceal it. I didn't want to deal with the fact I was going to be judged for who I was – nor did I want to go through any religious persecution from my church community as I was sure I was going to hear the "God loves you but hates the sin" lecture. After all, this was the message I had been hearing for most of my life at the church.

For many years, I hid in the closet and mastered keeping my sexual orientation a secret. It wasn't until I was 19 years old, during first year university, when I first came out to one of my friends. It was one of the toughest actions I had ever taken in my life, but it relieved so much of the bottled up 'self' that I was hiding. For the first time in a very long time, I was able to be myself again and I felt as if years and years of my 'unauthentic dirt' was being shed off of my skin. I knew from that moment on I had to continue coming out to my friends in order for me to be able to live a life that was fulfilling and well, just real.

I spent the next couple of years coming out to my friends and some coworkers. But the real difficult challenge I was faced with was coming out to my church and family members. By age 27, I had overcome some of these challenges and reached a point where I had told my siblings and my cousins (who are basically like my older sisters) and some of my church friends I had remained in contact with after I left the religious institution. Those were huge milestones in my 'coming out' journey and probably was just as difficult as coming out to my friend the very first time. As much as I told myself it didn't matter what others think of me, in fact, it really did matter whether the ones I was closest to by blood loved and accepted me for who I was.

After coming out to my siblings and cousins, I really struggled with whether or not to come out to my parents. By then, I had lived away from them for over ten years (my family had emigrated back to South Korea and I had left my parents to return to Canada when I was 16 years old) and I really felt there was no need to open a can of worms as long as we were living apart. "I could lie to them and they wouldn't know; they live on the other side of the world and hardly visit me anyway. I can get away with anything and everything I want and they will have absolutely no idea." A huge part of me wanted to protect them from the truth because I knew it would shake up their worldview as devout Christians and I also didn't want them to lose face amongst their friends in the Korean community – both inside and outside of the church. Ultimately, I knew that it would thwart my parents' life-long dreams and expectations of their eldest daughter and I really didn't want to disappoint or hurt them.

After my relationship with my first girlfriend didn't work out, I had an epiphany while reflecting on my life and my own happiness: I was thinking about how fragile life was and how every day was not my own to claim as it was not guaranteed. And then I was struck by the thought that if fate were to come knocking at my door and I were to suddenly die tomorrow (*knock on wood*), everybody at my funeral would know who I really was except for my very own parents – and that realization was just heartbreaking to me. The last thing I wanted was for my own living parents to not know who they gave birth to and I no longer wanted to be held down by any shame about who I was. I knew in my heart that God created me this way for a purpose – even though her purpose is taking a longer time than I would like for her fan club to understand. And so, the summer I was turning 28, I chose to visit my parents in South Korea for two weeks with the mission of coming out to them. I knew it was going to be the most difficult thing I was ever going to do in my life, but I also took comfort and courage in knowing that I was blessed with parents that were very loving and were not the type to disown their children, no matter what we said or did. And I know this is not the case for a lot of LGBTQ people's parents. Within the two week visit, I managed to muster up the courage to tell my parents the truth. Although I was right about the news upsetting them, I also knew it was my responsibility to share with them about who I was and now it was up to them to come to terms with it. By not sharing the truth with them, I was making my parents small – as if they couldn't handle who I was. I was taking away their ability to grow as human beings and to develop another layer of understanding of who their daughter was.

Feeling different is not always easy; especially when you're discovering this from a young age or as a teenager when the pressure to conform to your peers and parental/cultural expectations are always trumping your own desires to live your life authentically. The difficulty with sexual identity is that, unlike your ethnicity or abilities, it is hidden. One has to feel safe enough to come out to the person standing in front of them and declare who they are attracted to. In a world where heteronormativity and, often times, homophobia persists, this 'coming out' process to another human being can be a daunting task – especially when feeling like you're all alone.

The impact of being in the closet for as long as I could remember was that I fell into deep depression for all of my teenage years which was filled with self-hatred and suicidal thoughts, and this carried over to my early adulthood life. I was feeling increasingly suffocated and experienced self-hate for who I was and everything else that was different about me. What was worse was that I started to become distant from those that I loved because I felt so ashamed of my in-authenticity with others (never mind the fact that I was interested in other women), and they had no idea why I was pushing them away. If I could turn back the hours of time, I would have come out to my family and friends much sooner instead of enduring the periods of loneliness and self-hatred. However, I am a firm believer of everything happening for a reason. It was meant to be and I was born who I am. I believe I should share my story, so that the next young Korean adolescent going through this internal struggle of coming out to his/her loved ones knows that it doesn't have to be a battle they fight on their own.

To this day, my family members are still coming to terms with my sexual orientation and are at differing points of expressing their love and acceptance of who I am. I continue to share with them about my life and current partner, so I no longer withhold parts of myself from them. I recognize it is not always easy for them to hear, see, or understand this. I know that this was all meant to be part of my journey, as well as theirs – and where I am, right now, is perfect.

~ Esther Kim ~

Photo: Pune Camp, India, by Elisa De Pascali

Passion over Past

In 2006, I was arrested without explanation by the Islamic authorities in Iran. Later I was told I was being accused of using my social project as a way to convert Muslim children to the Baha'i Faith. The Baha'i Faith is an independent religion not recognized by the Iranian government. The social program I ran was transparent and both Baha'i's and Muslims were working together to serve our little brother's and sister's to provide them with free education. But the Islamic government was skeptical. After weeks of hearings in the court, the judge dropped the charges of 'attempting to organize illegal groups to rebel against the government of Iran' and 'cooperating with other groups to undermine the central government.' But since I was not allowed to have a lawyer, I was found guilty for teaching the Baha'i' Faith and sentenced to four years in prison. I passed three years and four months in an isolation cell (individual prison) and the remaining eight months in a 'hidden' prison.

The isolation cell was a small chamber with a lavatory. The iron door was always closed and there were no windows. Food was passed to me through a little window on the door. In my cell there was a heater, a cooler, and 3 blankets. Other things I had in my cell were: soap, shampoo, a tooth brush, tooth paste, a box of handkerchiefs, a nail trimmer, a box of detergent, a towel, a comb and one shirt. Everyday prisoners could have a 15-20 minute walk in the yard outside. There were no trees or grass in the yard; only a concrete floor (as wide as a volleyball court) and high walls. The only beauty visible was the beautiful blue sky above. When the weather was too hot, too cold or rainy you were not allowed out for fresh air. Once a week prisoners could meet and talk to her/his family by phone behind thick glass for five minutes.

It took me one week to learn how I should manage myself without falling into a tormented routine. I spent my time praying, reading books, exercising, walking in the cell and watching TV. But I only got these privileges after I wrote many letters to the head of the prison. For the first eight months, they did not follow the prisoner rights. They didn't give me any books, magazines, paper or pens. For almost one year they didn't even give me my glasses without which I constantly had blurred vision. I wrote to the warden saying if he will not follow the prisoner rights at least follow human rights. We had many meetings and over time, I slowly got privileges.

While I was in solitary confinement for forty months in the Intelligence prison in Shiraz, I was given the option to write a 'forgiveness plea' so that I could get released early. I declined to write the plea because I was not guilty, so as 'real' punishment, I was sent to Adel Abad Prison for the remaining eight months of my sentence. Adel Abad prison was for men only, but there was a 'hidden' prison inside for troublemaking women who were sentenced to life in prison or had a death penalty. For those eight months my cell was an old kitchen. I shared a 6 square metre room with 11 other female inmates who were murderers, smugglers, sex trafficking victims and drug dealers. There was a concrete floor with one small mat. A large part of the roof was missing so we felt the rain, the cold and the sun. Mosquitoes and mice were everywhere and there was lots of lice. There was no shower, an open toilet with no plumbing, no warm water and no hygienic supplies. I did not receive food or drinking water for the first three days, and on the third day they brought eight cooked turnips to share. The guards used to illegally supply the women with drugs (heroin, crystal methamphetamine and opium) so they were inattentive and a mess. After a few days, I wrote a letter to the prison warden describing the conditions of the cell. Even though the guard discouraged this, saying I would be severely punished, I insisted he deliver the letter. I was called to the warden's office and he asked about my 'nonsense' letter. I told him it was not nonsense and invited him to come and see the cell with his own eyes. He asked why I was in prison and after I explained, the guard retrieved my file, which was only one sheet of paper. On the paper it was written that I was a spy, and a Muslim converted to Christianity. He showed me the paper and at the bottom it said I was to be banned from contact or from speaking to anyone. He then asked me questions about Baha'i beliefs, and we ended up having an hour long conversation. In that hour the warden's demeanor changed – he started to soften. He then came with me to see the conditions of my cell.

The next day a shower was installed; they repaired the plumbing, and covered the hole in the roof. They provided one shampoo and one bar of soap to share, blankets, and drinking water. One day, a fight broke out among the women over a small piece of opium. The guards entered and started beating these women with batons. They took all of them away for drug testing, body searches and interrogation. I remember getting emotional and wept. A guard asked me why the tears, and I said, that my heart was broken from seeing this, because I couldn't understand why I was here, in this mess! The guard believed my innocence and exempted me from the interrogation, drug testing and body search. I watched as ten of the women tested positive for narcotics and were sentenced to 30 backlashes each. I spoke up, despite my tears, and asked if they could be given the opportunity to quit and if they were unsuccessful, then the punishment could be carried out. Although the guards refused my request at this time, the warden walked in and asked what was going on. I repeated my request and he said, "No". After much begging from the women the warden agreed to give them one week to quit, but if they did not become clean, they would receive the 30 backlashes and so would I. No medical assistance was provided for these women to quit; I took care of them all by myself. I fed them, bathed them and after one week they were re-tested. Nine of the women were clean, and the other two didn't pass the test; not because they had resumed drugs, but because they had too many drugs in their system. The punishment was never carried out.

In the coming weeks, the women began fighting with each other because they were drug free and alert, but had nothing to do. I wrote another letter to the warden suggesting that he provide some kind of job opportunity to keep them busy. When the warden asked 'what kind of work,' I suggested a sewing workshop. It took 3 weeks, but my request was approved. One day, the guards took us all out of the room. When we returned three days later, the entire room had changed! The walls were painted, there were tables, sewing machines, benches, cutting tables, lights, supplies, materials and a pant patterns. The first week we were asked to make 20 pairs of pants. Many of the women did not know how to use the machines, so I divided sewing tasks according to their skills and capabilities. After the warden approved our work, he ordered us to make another 20 pairs, good enough quality to sell. After a few weeks the number increased to 50 pairs of pants.

I continued to write letters and make requests, and over time most were granted; we got a small refrigerator, an air conditioner, a television, and a hot plate for cooking. When my request to have books was denied, I decided to listen and write down the stories of the women instead. It was interesting because these women wanted to talk about themselves and their tough life. So when I asked them to talk to me, they accepted whole heartedly.

Many people might think that living with little facilities is very difficult, but one can learn how to live with minimal facilities without any problem. How you train your spirit and mind to think about the values of humanity, spirituality and divine goals is what's important. In this way, I became glad, thankful, and enjoyed the opportunities I had in prison.

You may also think that being in the prison is hard and sad, but if you believe that patience and perseverance in misfortunes is the cause of spiritual progress and elevation of the individual, it gives you pleasure. In spite of the fact that some days being in prison was hard for me, whenever I think about the time I passed there, I get a feeling of spiritual joy! The days in prison gave me many important lessons and it has made me ready for giving more services to the human world. During this time, especially the last eight months, I learned much about managing people; dividing work, pointing out errors, correcting them and using people's talents. I also learned project management skills, like how to begin, develop and finish a project successfully. I also helped people to communicate better, even when they didn't get along.

Little by little, I saw change in people. The women became more confident even though most would never see life outside the prison and some were sentenced to die. The attitude of the prison guards toward the women changed; over time they showed them respect and treated them like humans. The prison warden softened and granted most of my requests which allowed me to create a space and give these women power. I think the biggest lesson I learned was; if you observe a situation very carefully, you will learn that you can change the environment and change society. Your framework of thoughts should be to change the situation, not to give up on it whether it is good or bad. You should be a light wherever you are, and I saw going to prison as an opportunity to be a light.

~ *Raha Sabet Sarvestany* ~

"Be your own good example of perseverance. We've all had days that seemed catastrophic, but we managed to overcome those moments and carry on. Focus on your good qualities and use them: Take stock of your accomplishments and allow them to propel you forward."

~ Alena Dervisevic ~

When I was 13 years old, two boys sexually assaulted me. These boys were the sons of a family friend who were living at our home for a period of time. Although I endured the abuse for months, I chose not tell on them. Then one day, on what seemed to be the sunniest day that summer, they cornered me in my room and raped me.

Since my first experience of physical intimacy was with them, countless feelings and thoughts came to mind. Is this love? Why didn't I stop them? Is this my fault? Those same thoughts and feelings lingered in my head for years after.

At one point later in life, I confronted those boys about the incident, to which they replied that I was crazy and completely over exaggerating. Since no one else knew about the situation, I believed them.

The experiences affected my entire lifestyle – the people I talked to, the places I went, the clothes I wore and the things I did. Looking back, I can see how my demeanor changed because of those incidences. But during my teen years, I really thought everything was okay. I thought being physically intimate with someone was the only way people could show love to each other. So what if I occasionally had nightmares about my male friends assaulting me? So what if I didn't like hugs? I thought it was normal.

It wasn't until my mid to late teens that I confided the incidences to my boyfriend at the time. He convinced me to tell my pastors, with whom I started counseling sessions. It took them months to get through to me; to get me to realize that ignoring and suppressing these incidences were not going to make my life any easier. But understanding their perspective took time, and these counseling sessions continued for several months.

I can't really narrow down the day of my turning point. I know it was last spring, a couple months after my 25th birthday. One day I realized that no matter how good things were going for me, something was missing. I loved my job, my family, my friends, and I was actively going to church and the gym. I wasn't necessarily unhappy – I wouldn't even call it a hole – but you know how sometimes when you're writing an exam you skip a page and go on and complete the other pages first? I realized the page I kept skipping in my life was dealing with the sexual assault and rape. My adulthood was going well – I felt successful and happy. But when I tried to move forward and grow, it seemed almost impossible. After years of nightmares and a bitter distant attitude, I eventually realized it was those childhood experiences that were lingering in my present. And eventually it hit me; unless I dedicated the time and effort to confront these incidences, I would never be able to move onto that next step – whatever it was.

Gradually, I've become more open about the incidences. I've taken courses and talked to a few professionals and non-professionals about it. Although it's not easy, it's a topic I now choose not to shy away from because I think silence gives it power.

Last summer, I was listening to a show on CBC and the question came up as to whether or not the word 'sexual assault' should be used instead of the word 'rape' in the courtroom. With my entire body shaking, I called in as 'Samantha from Sarnia' and said I was raped when I was 13 years old. I indicated that for years I used the words 'sexual assault' instead of 'rape' because it seemed too powerful of a word – too explicit. But the jurors, the accused and the victims need to know that there is a difference between sexual assault and rape. While there are varying levels and definitions of sexual assault, in my opinion, rape's definition should never be questioned. Although I changed my name, this was the first time I really spoke publicly about my experience and took a stand for myself.

A few weeks later, I was speaking with my dad about something in the news and he mentioned the importance of outspoken people. He then said, "Yeah, just like Samantha in Sarnia." After a few seconds of silence on the phone, I responded by saying, "So umm, you heard me?" to which he replied, "Man, I am so proud of you. I love you so much."

This year (2015) marks thirteen years since the assault. I've come a long way, but there's still a ways to go. I'm a spiritual person and I believe that God's only going to reveal things to me one piece at a time; I just need to be patient. I'm sharing my testimony because I believe there is someone out there who needs to hear about this particular stage in my life at this particular time. As such, I am choosing not to give 'silence' the power.

~ Stephanie McLean ~

Photo: Wack N'gouna, Senegal, by Nilmi Senaratna

At 33, Tokyo born and residing in NYC I learned about Domestic Violence (DV). My counselor told me there are four main types of DV: physical, emotional, financial and sexual. I received all these types of violence from 2009 until 2011. My ex-husband followed the Cycle of Violence; he was depressed, angry, abusive and apologetic, and he repeated this cycle nonstop until I released myself from his life. I hope my story can help other women be aware of each type of DV and objectively understand The Cycle of Violence. We are Women – one of the most beautiful creatures in this Universe! I overcame my past, here is my story.

I met my husband in 2007 and we got married very happily in 2009. He had a beautiful 3-year-old son, and I was super grateful to be his step mother. We were all very peaceful and fun together until my husband broke his wrist badly at work. He lost his jobs (he had several artistic talents) and the small contracting business he started. Losing his right hand did major damage to him, and this is when I slowly started to experience the full set of domestic violence.

After breaking his wrist he became very depressed. He would get angry easily and had trouble sleeping. When he got angry, he would put me down and yell at me to leave him alone. It seemed like I could never talk to him without upsetting him. He was helpless; I had to help him bathe, get dressed, and I made all his meals. I had a full-time job, housework and worked hard to support us both while also caring for his son. By the time the cast came off, he had become lazy. He went to physical therapy for his wrist but he didn't do the exercises. He gave up his old jobs and started to rely on me financially.

I learned I was pregnant and his behavior got worse. One day we had a huge argument about money. He screamed at me, grabbed me and shoved me to the floor – knowing full well that I was pregnant. I landed hard and pain shot up my lower back. I struggled to get to my feet, and once up, I went to the freezer and got ice for my back. I lied on the sofa in pain and that's when he came over to me. By this time he had calmed down and said he was sorry, but he started becoming affectionate with me. I was still scared and in shock about what he had just done, but I was even more afraid that if I pushed him away he would resume his angry rage. So I laid there while he had sex with me even though I was still in a lot of pain. Once he got up and went to his home office, I laid there crying. It got to the point where he often had sex with me against my will, especially when I was in pain. I felt I had no choice because I feared he would greatly hurt me if I did not agree. I decided after this incident I could not bring a baby into this violent situation, so on September 1st, 2009, I got an abortion.

As the months passed, I became very exhausted and tense, both physically and mentally. I was working full-time and taking care of the house, my husband and his son. My husband spent most of his time in his home office. He slept during the day and was awake at night. We barely saw each other and communicated even less. Often, he locked the office door so I could not reach him. I had to call or text him in order for us to communicate. To cope, I invested all my time into his son and focused on keeping him happy. I truly loved that boy. He was an angel to me.

When the finances got worst, I had a conversation with my husband about getting a part-time job to help with the bills. He refused, saying he was 'trying hard' and 'doing his best!' Every time I asked for his help, he became aggressive and shouted. He punched walls and made holes in the low-ceiling, so eventually I just stopped talking to him about the bills. When not being aggressive, he completely ignored me. I was becoming home sick and more and more lonely. I was stressed and tired from being overworked. I tried to talk with him about my feelings, but he was always busy, tired or said, "we'll talk tomorrow." He had shut me out and no longer talked to me about anything. I felt I was his slave. No freedom and no love from the one who I loved most.

At one point, my husband told me he wanted us to have an 'open relationship'. I had no idea what that was and didn't respond. He took that to mean that I was okay with it, and started to bring women home and was openly affectionate with them in front of me. I was so upset, but I had nowhere to go. I lost my strength of mind and accepted whatever he wanted. During this time I had lost my appetite. I was about 11 pounds below my normal weight and at one point I weighed 92 pounds. I had insomnia and really bad acne, and because of stress, I got an ulcer in my oesophagus.

The last time my husband was physically abusive was on March 31st, 2011, and it was also the most violent abuse I suffered. We were arguing about money, and I followed him into the bedroom to continue the conversation. He then suddenly came up to me, grabbed me and shoved me onto the floor. My head hit the table on the way down and I landed on my back. I was crying in pain, and my husband said it was my fault, but then his behavior completely changed, he started acting sweet and friendly. He began caressing my head – he was interested in having sex. I was terrified and didn't want to have sex at all. As I got up to get away, I tripped over the cord of the floor lamp he used for photo shoots, and it crashed to the floor. He became enraged again so I ran out from my house to my neighbor's house. I waited there over night until I could safely get my belongings.

The next day, I went to the emergency room to treat my head injury. The doctor asked how I got the injury and I told him what happened. This was the first time I told anyone about the abuse. The doctor asked if I wanted to report it to the police, but I said no. I didn't want to make my husband upset or make things worse. Also, I didn't want to make him sad; after all, I still loved him. Then the doctor asked if I wanted to divorce my husband, and to this I said, "Yes I want a divorce…" I realized then for the first time I was being honest with myself. The doctor told me I had to start collecting the evidence of his abuse. I was shocked and scared but with the help of a social worker at the hospital, I chose to take the first step and I called the police to report the incident and filed a claim with Victim Services.

On April 8th, 2011, my husband was arrested. I received an order of protection from the criminal court and was given information about the New York Asian Women's Centre, which helps victims of domestic violence, and a week later I began counseling. My counselor has supported me and helped me understand what I had gone through with my ex-husband. I know it is important to discuss and work through what happened even though it's not easy. Since I left my husband and house, it has taken me some time to get back on my feet emotionally, physically and financially, but I am happy with the new life I started and now share with my dog.

I couldn't take action for a long time because I forgot how to feel my heart. I forgot how to take care of myself because I prioritized my husband and his son – always living for others and not for me. While I care about others, I see now I need to take care of myself too. Staying equal all the time and finding that balance is still a challenge for me, but it's getting better.

I don't feel pain in my heart anymore. I have always been a very bright and talkative person, so I don't know how I let myself drown for so long. But, I overcame the dark time and I am at peace and live a healthy life again. This experience taught me a lot so now I say, "Thank you Universe for this experience!" I'm mastering happiness, and like the meaning of my name, Sachiyo – 'Goddess of Happiness' – I am a student of the Universe; an important one like everyone, pure like a child, lively like a tree, changing like the ocean waves, light like dark, positive like negative and future like past. We are all connected, so let go and be free.

You are the only one who can master your life, and I see this now as a fun challenge! Creating profound meaning every single moment, with all kinds of beings and environments; that is the true process of happiness and choice, is a powerful thing!

~ Sachi* ~

At 19 years old I weighed 274 pounds. I ate whatever I wanted, whenever I wanted, with no regard to what I was doing to my body. I would drink apple juice from the can, I mean why waste time with a cup right? A few mouthfuls and the whole thing was gone – this was a daily occurrence. As was my French fries ritual. But was I embarrassed or ashamed of this behavior? Nope, not even for a second. I was uneducated about food and I thought this is who I was meant to be. I had tried every fad diet out there and nothing worked (well lets be honest, it's because I still ate what I wanted… or I was 'good' for only a few days at a time).

As I said, I thought that this was my life and I was destined to be fat. Even fat is too nice of a word, I was obese. I would live in sweatpants and sweaters even in the heat of the summer because I thought I was fooling people. When I look back I see that the only person I was fooling was myself.

Things started to get real when I was lying in bed at night and couldn't breathe because the weight was too heavy for my own lungs. I couldn't move and chaffing happened even in the winter. I was miserable. So in a feeble attempt to get healthy I joined a gym in November 2007. I started out slowly with my exercise program, but then used that as an excuse to eat more… you know since I had 'worked out' and all.

One night at the gym, I saw a Weight Watchers meeting was starting so I decided to sit in the very back and listen to what they said. It seemed pretty good so I joined right then and there. No 'starting on Monday' and when Monday rolls around wait until the next week. I had committed – and by committed I mean paid money so I knew I had to at least try. And that is what I did. I tried. I thought "I will give the program an honest try (even though I knew it wouldn't work)." I went home and I had my mom take my 'before' picture.

My first week on the program I lost 4 pounds. WHAAAAT? 4 pounds in my first week?! Okay... maybe this might work. I kept attending weekly meetings and I slowly started to learn about food, what it does to our bodies, and how to eat properly. I also learned that I could still have the foods that I loved I just had to have them in moderation. No more six pack of donuts on the way home from work and before eating dinner. As I started to lose the weight things started to become easier. I started to move and breathe better, and for the first time EVER I could cross my legs!

If I had to look back and say what I remember the most about losing weight, I would say it was when I reached the '40 pounds gone' mark. I didn't see a difference in myself when I looked in the mirror everyday but I compared a picture of myself to my before picture and I could finally start to see it. I could see the work I was accomplishing and for the first time I truly believed "This is going to work!"

I kept plugging away at my weight loss. I continued to learn about my body and my weight loss patterns. I learned how to make the food I loved in a much healthier way and I was doing activities I never dreamed I'd be able to do like play tennis and canoe. I incorporated physical fitness into my daily routine where ever possible. I started out doing just cardio, but now one of the things I am most passionate about is strength training with weights and metabolic workouts – on top of my beloved cardio of course. Choosing to be passionate about working out saved my health. I even got back into playing competitive soccer, which I had to give up because I just couldn't keep up anymore.

It was not always easy – in fact there were many times that I wanted to quit. I used to get mad that I couldn't eat the way I used to eat and still lose weight and be healthy at the same time. But one thing stuck with me (I am really big on analogies, they help me stay focused everyday) and that was I used to be jealous of the people who could move around, tie their shoes, and cross their legs. Now I was jealous of my old self who hid behind mountains of food. I couldn't have it both ways. I decided right then and there that my old self was nothing to be jealous of – and my new self was something to be very proud of. I am committed to never going back!

From start to finish I lost 115 pounds, and I worked very hard for every one of those! Now I can do things I never dreamed I would be able to do – including climbing numerous mountains (literally, climbing mountains). So many things are open to me now that I wouldn't have had the chance to do before, including chasing my little girl around and actually being able to keep up!

My heart hurts when I see people where I used to be. I know exactly what they are going through and I feel their pain. If they could feel, even for a day, the empowerment and strength I feel every day now from making healthy choices and living an active lifestyle, they would get to experience firsthand how amazing life is! I am not saying life can't be amazing when you are overweight, but if you have lost weight before and feel what I feel every time I do so many squats that I can't walk, then you would know what I mean. I am far from perfect, and I still overdo it with eating the wrong things sometimes – but this is a life long journey, one that I am happy to be a part of.

YOU are the only person who can control what goes in your mouth. You might think you are making healthy choices, but you have no idea the hidden culprits in your food that are working against you. You have the power to change your diet and work towards a healthy lifestyle. Put down the chips (at least for now), get off the couch, and take that first step. Make a commitment today, because tomorrow is never a guarantee.

~ Kelly McNamara ~

My story could probably be summarized as this: wrong relationship with the wrong person. I was dating a guy and although I loved him, I was not open to seeing that he did not love me back – that he was not a good guy and that he was using me. I stopped calling him and he did the same with me but after a month, I felt the need to see him again. Not to 'hang out', that's for sure. Honestly, I did not know what I wanted. Maybe, 'clarification', just to put an end point to that stupid relationship. So we met and it was a disaster! He acted goofy and insensitive, which only irritated me more, but then we had a huge fight and for the very first time, he hit me.

I vividly remember that night; on my way home, I felt like scratching the bottom of a barrel. Although I had no bruises, I felt devastated and broken. This incident happened a few days before my birthday, and I never told my family or my friends about it. I wanted to forget about it – to erase that episode and that story from my memories. But not being able to, I then put all my effort and dedication into my studies and I started to act controlling in every aspect of my life. I became depressed and anxious. Panic attacks started to surprise me in the most unexpected situations. I became obsessed with food and my studies; I wanted to be perfect and have full control of every factor in my life. I did not feel like seeing people anymore. In a way I wanted to, but I was scared to get out and face the world. I felt weak and fragile, as if I was made of glass.

Then LOVE saved me. The passionate feelings I have for my family and my best friends is what got me through it. Although my family and friends did not fully understand my drama, they were there for me. I realized I would not have been able to fight that battle by myself and I decided to trust them and accept their help. LOVE is strong and little by little, I started to trust people again. After that incident, I had completely lost faith in human beings and my ability to put all the pieces together. It was not easy, but I was totally determined to rise and move on.

That episode happened twelve years ago, and although I have a scar of violence and abuse within me, I continue to grow stronger and happier. I've become more courageous and more determined to challenge myself. I even decided to not live a simple life and to follow my heart and my passions. Love is also part of that. Life is wonderful; an amazing trip that is worth sharing with the people you care about. Do not forget about them and let them help you whenever you cannot make it by yourself. Love, Passion and Family are truly healing.

~ Anonymous ~

Photo: Pune Camp, India, by Elisa De Pascali

Seventeen years after the incident, it continues to have an impact on my sexual relations.

I had just turned 13 when I went on a fencing competition with my Berlin Fencing Club. The competition took place not far from Berlin. Our team had to spend one night in a youth hostel. Older age groups were fighting on Saturday. I was the youngest on our team and my tournament was scheduled on Sunday.

After the first day of the tournament, we went to a restaurant and then back to our hostel. I shared my room with two older girls. In order to be in good physical condition for the tournament the next day, I went to bed early. We were sleeping on two bunk beds; the other girls each on one of the beds below and I was sleeping on the bed above. Before drifting off, I remember the two girls chatting in our room with some boy from our fencing team. I was not very interested in their conversation and soon fell asleep.

I always sleep on my stomach, so I do not remember if the boy stayed in the room until both girls fell asleep, or if he came back later. But what I do remember is that I heard the squeak of my ladder while he came up to my bed. He was two years older than me. I remember him – he was tall and strong. I was 13, and did not know what was going on. I had never kissed a boy; I had not even had my first menstruation yet, so I still felt like a child, not a teenager.

He came up to me and laid his body on mine. He was heavy. I remember that he tried to pull down my pants, but

I was pressing myself against the mattress. Then he started moving his hips; harder, faster, and more and more intense. I felt his penis on my buttocks – it was hard, uncomfortable and he was heavy. He came on me. I felt disgusted and disgusting. Then, he left. During the entire incident we did not exchange any words.

Later, I did not understand why I did not speak up. Why I did not scream? Why I did not ask for help from one of the other girls in the room. I must have been in some sort of shock or denial.

The next day, the boy did not talk to me. I tried to be nice and friendly, but he disregarded me. I remember that I did not understand what was going on. I was puzzled and thought I might have made a mistake. He continued going to the same training lessons as me, and we were going to the same school, which meant that I had to see him every day for the next few years.

Now I am 30 years old, and all of my boyfriends have treated me nicely and with respect. Nonetheless, I had to share this incident with each of them; otherwise they would not understand my flashbacks and my sudden shivers while making love. It only dawns on me now that this boy laid the foundation for all my future sexual relations with men. Although he is not part of my daily life anymore, the memories remain vivid.

Until a few weeks ago, I was convinced that this incident happened when I was 16 years old, but recently I checked my diary collection from when I was a child and it is only now that I realize how young I really was. In my diary I explicitly explain the tournament, but I did not write anything about what happened during the night. What stunned me the most was that after that day, I stopped writing in my diary for at least six months. Prior to that I wrote daily.

Since I was very young, I have been fighting for other people's rights (as a class representative, as one of the founders of the youth parliament in Berlin, as a founder and president of an NGO which helps to empower women in West Africa). And now I am finishing my Phd, which develops a strategy on how to fight Female Genital Mutilation and oppression of women.

I feel now I can fight for my own rights; to stand up and help the young girl in me to heal. Writing this testimony for the Passion over Past book project was my first step.

~ Hanna ~

Self-esteem

related to my body image has stretched into several facets of my life. When I was a child, I was overweight and had skin problems. At home my parents alienated me, and because of their actions it influenced my siblings to do the same. To this day I do not know why I was the outcast, but I think it was because I was ugly, fat and stupid. In tenth grade, I remember faking the grades on my report card to see if that would make my parents love me, and when that didn't work, I gave up on school.

School life was my home situation magnified! I did not live up to the high academic standards most people expected from Asians and for that reason people made fun of me. I was only invited to parties because without me, my sister would not be able to attend. The last party I ever went to involved an organized session of horrendous name-calling and humiliation. Since my sister was already predisposed to alienating me, she joined in with others. They threw cigarette butts at me and called me 'Roseanne' (the comedian Roseanne Bar). The bullying was unbearable.

At one point, I decided to stop crying about being fat and ugly and chose to do something about it. My best friend was the President of the Boys Athletic Association and a star athlete. I asked him to help me lose weight by teaching me how to run properly and play basketball. By the time grade twelve started, I had lost so much weight that people started to notice and treat me differently. The attention was nice, but I admit that I cheated. For the entire month of August, I only ate food portions the size of ¼ of one of my fists and after I ate, I forced myself to vomit. I also barely drank water since in my mind, water would swell my body. I went from 159 to 109 pounds in a matter of weeks. I was numb to any sort of shame I could have felt about my habits because the results where exactly what I wanted. Dropping the waistline was my bottom line! That same year, I played a prank on an ex-friend who was always making fun of me. Although I succeeded in humiliating her, I ended up getting kicked out of high school and charged with physical assault. Ultimately, I never finished high school.

I moved into a place of my own but was bad with money thanks to my obsession with night life – the clubs, the drinks, and the guys. Many mornings I woke up on the kitchen floor since I was too intoxicated to get to my bed. I bartended at night and during the day I had this habit of drinking a bottle of wine at lunch, passing out and waking up in time for my shift at the dive bar. Additionally, my boss at the bar encouraged drinking on the job so we used to do shots on the hour, every hour. Denial is easy with a shot of whisky!

One night while working, I met a man eight years older than me. He seemed mature and responsible so we started dating, and like most new relationships, all was fine. He would tell me that we were 'meant to be' because we both came from the same kind of bullied upbringing, and this made me feel connected to him – like I had finally found someone who understood me. I supported us while he pursued his career as a comedian full-time. I moved in with him in his dark, filthy basement apartment filled with cigarette smoke. Being a comedian meant a lot of nights at bars and a lot of drinking, and excessive drinking often led to aggressive arguments.

One night after having drinks at a bar somewhere on College Street, we got into a huge fight. Once back at the apartment, the arguing turned into domestic abuse. I vividly remember him being on top of me – his knee on my throat and chest, pressing so hard that I couldn't breathe. He whispered in my ear, "I know how to choke a person without leaving marks so even if you charge me you have no proof." Despite those words, I decided to forgive him. I told myself it was my fault anyway and, not surprising, he agreed. We had an on-and-off relationship for another year and the abuse continued; one night he pinned me to a wall, choked me and punched me three times in the stomach. Along with the regular partying I started to do a lot of cocaine, and I mean A LOT. Eventually, I lost both of my restaurant jobs because I got into a fight with a girl at a bar. My life was a mess.

The stress about money, rent and food were really getting to me. Shortly after I started working part-time at a vintage shop, I started to get stomach aches. A few weeks later, I was hospitalized for five days. After some tests, and not eating for three days, the doctors told me I had developed diverticulitis – an abscess that grows on the wall of the large intestine. I was told that I was too young to have this condition and stress was likely the cause.

After being diagnosed with diverticulitis, I started to follow an all-natural way of living. This alternative lifestyle helped me in such a tremendous way! I stopped eating out and became passionate about preparing my own delicious, green meals at home. I was hooked on learning about herbal medicine and trying to incorporate that in my everyday life by making my own shampoo, conditioner, face and body wash. When my best friend got pregnant, I looked up minerals, vitamins, organic vegetables and fruits that would be good for her to eat during her pregnancy. Sharing my findings in plant medicine and clean eating, made me feel really good – like I was making a difference! I felt great being able to help people get their health on track. It actually reminded me how at one time I considered pursuing a career in public healthcare.

In March 2014, my best friend gave birth to Zara and announced that she wanted me to be the Godmother! This new all-natural life was leading to beautiful and positive changes. After Zara was born, I decided that I was not going to let my past dictate my future. I decided to take online courses, get my high school diploma and apply to college for dental hygiene. Not only did I realize that I could pursue this desire to work in public healthcare, but I wanted to make sure I could be the cool Godmother that could fund extracurricular activities or school trips for Zara. I wanted to make sure I could help her with school tuition and books when that day comes. And I especially wanted to be ready for when I have my own children.

I've had an amazing experience turning my life around and practicing an all-natural way of life. I have learned to love myself more than I ever have before. There's a special connection with nature that makes me feel like I have everything I could ever need around me. It was really rewarding for me to look back and reflect on all the things that made me feel like I wasn't going to be beautiful, healthy, smart and strong. Now I see I am all of those things thanks to the help of organic produce, plant medicine and the kind, wonderful people who have shared their research and testimonials. I am proud to say I have reached my ideal healthy weight, my skin glows and looks young and fresh, and I'm getting A's on my assignments and tests through my online courses. Lastly, I have successfully applied to college for dental hygiene. I did not let my bad choices and sad past break me down because I am resilient! Even though I had an abusive ex-boyfriend in the past, I did not close my heart to love. Now I have a truly wonderful man in my life and that's just the beginning! The many years of insecurities, substance abuse, heartache and loneliness slowly faded away the minute I decided to take control of my life and do it the way that made sense to me. I used to think I was too old to start over but now I definitely know that it's never too late to plant seeds and watch them grow.

> *I never was athletic but I could go the distance and jump over obstacles, because I believed.*

~ Su Tran ~

While pursuing my post-graduate studies, I was sexually harassed by my graduate school supervisor. The experience began as a subtle manipulative tactic, but developed into a forthright abusive relationship. Although I was only directly in the situation for eleven months, the weight and the effects caused by the incident lasted much longer.

For over two years, I would unexpectedly burst into tears and found myself unable to stop. I felt bruised and beaten, though I had not been physically touched. I was constantly nauseated but had no signs or symptoms of illness. Above all, I feared everyone – always questioning my intelligence, my actions and my reason for being. My brain and body was spent; I found even the smallest tasks exhausting, strenuous and overwhelming. I would rise in the morning only to nap again soon after. I ate if I remembered to, but I had lost my appetite for both food and life. My hair fell out in clumps, while my face was overcome with acne. I lost my interest in things that once brought me joy and I purposely excluded myself from social gatherings and avoided friends. During the night I would rise in terror – gasping for air, unable to breath, feeling as though I were being strangled. Anxiety accompanied my every emotion. It chaperoned my mood and my thoughts, while continually suppressing my confidence, my personality and my 'joie de vivre'. And though surrounded by people, I felt completely alone. Family and friends showed support, but I felt like sharing was pointless since they simply did not understand. Smiling was a painful chore and laughing was an empty act. Nothing made sense; I was the victim, yet scolded for being the cause in this matter. I felt used, unwanted and embarrassed – drowning in shallow water, traumatized by the idea that my life had no purpose and my future had been ruined.

This was the darkest time of my life, and I felt that my existence was beyond what I could see at that point in time. I had no idea where I was going or how I was going to get out, but what was clear to me was that I could not stay where I was. The ongoing problem I faced was that I did not have the mental capacity or confidence to keep myself motivated. When I took the necessary steps to move forward, I found myself confronted, and fell back into a state of fear and helplessness. I remember waking up and telling myself, "Ok, lets take action today", then the smallest incident would force me back into a state of depression. This continued for several months until a small, simple activity came into my life and transformed me forever: Running.

One beautiful sunny spring day, I found myself sitting outside my favorite café in Ottawa. The sun was refreshing, the air was warm and as I sat on the patio, I received a text from a friend requesting to meet up. Not long after, my friend Greg approached my table in sweaty gym clothes with a medal around his neck. His presence was illuminating and I could instantly feel his energy. With a giant smile he indicated that he had just finished running the Ottawa marathon. While I was speechless by his extraordinary accomplishment, Greg mentioned had he been more consistent in his training, he likely would have done better, but thanks to *The Running Room* he completed his goal. Never having heard of The Running Room, Greg highlighted the benefits of running with a group. As he raved about the pros, I remember being dumbfounded by the whole concept. I could not envision hundreds of people willing to meet up at a specified location multiple times a week, simply to run. This I had to see for myself. At this point, I recall my concentration had shifted to the shiny piece of hardware hanging by Greg's chest. My eyes were locked on the blue ribbon around his neck which clearly stated 'marathon finisher'. Without a peep, I sat back in my chair, and after looking up at the sky I thought to myself, "I want to be a marathon finisher." In that moment the world fell quiet and I made a simple promise to myself. I had no idea how I was going to do it, but for the first time in months I had only one thought in my head and it was now clear – I was going to run the Ottawa marathon the following year. And so this was the start of my transformation; a new life began.

The following May, I found myself standing at a starting line among thousands of other runners. I vividly remember the excitement that filled the air that cool Sunday morning and the disbelief I felt in reading the banner which read "Welcome to the 2013 Tamarack Ottawa Marathon." As runners exchanged smiles, hugs and 'good luck' wishes, I stood among the crowd in silence. With my hands together in prayer and my head bowed, I closed my eyes and felt a tear slowly stream down my cheek. A feeling of pride overcame my being and I found myself overcome with joy. I had yet to take a step, but I felt like I had already finished. A year ago running a marathon seemed like an outrageous impossibility, yet there I was surrounded by my running friends, confident in my ability to run 42.2 kilometres. After making this promise to myself that sunny spring afternoon, my life took a positive turn and it has remained so ever since.

Throughout my running career, I have participated in many races, some reaching the lengths of 50 kilometres. I've met the most fascinating and loving people; all have been supportive and a source of inspiration throughout my journey. I've transformed my diet and exercise regimen while dabbling in new hobbies like trekking. Only three months after running the Ottawa marathon I reached the Uhuru summit peak of Mount Kilimanjaro – the tallest free-standing mountain in the world. And this is just the tip of the iceberg. My life has blossomed in ways I had never considered possible prior to being harassed. A few years ago, the vision for my life included finishing graduate school, becoming an intern at Parliament and settling into a comfortable government job. Today, I have a graduate degree in 'being unstoppable!' I am a self-expressed life-coach, standing for the transformation of others. I consistently train to accomplish extravagant adventures and overall I am living a life I love! Running did not transform my life; rather it empowered my understanding of choice, and to be someone other than a victim of sexual harassment. By adopting a new mindset and choosing to be someone beyond the person I was during that experience, I have discovered a new way of being and a new purpose for my life. Inspired, committed, engaged, refreshed and energized, in choosing to be a runner, I now see my life as a miraculous gift!

~ Laska Paré ~

The Power of Choice

When I chose to start running, the first step I committed to was 'showing up'. At that time, I was broken. All tasks were arduous, so small simple steps were all I could handle. I remember telling myself that first night... "Just get to the running club. You don't even have to run, just get there!" While I managed to get dressed and out the door, I was terrified. After months of isolation, I was headed to a public setting, surrounded by people I did not know, attempting an activity I did not do. Yet, one's greatest growth comes during their greatest discomfort. Although I was uncomfortable, at that time I knew I did not need comfort, I needed growth; a step away from where I was. To my surprise when I arrived at the running club that night, I was warmly greeted by the runners and staff. I fulfilled my commitment of 'showing up' and the result of that action led to a community of friendly people. Initially I did not intend to run, but since my first action led to a 'good' result (friendly people) I was curious to see where the next action would lead. Although I was breathless and could barely keep up, after finishing the second action (running), to my surprise the result again was 'good'. Since the results of my actions were seemingly 'positive', I chose to show up at the running club again that Sunday, and as they say, the rest is history!

Looking back, 'showing up' was unknowingly the first step I took in becoming an Ultra Runner. Note that there was nothing Hollywood or picturesque about that first night, nor did I start running and instantly discover a hidden running talent – quite the opposite, I felt like my lungs were going to explode! But as previously mentioned, running did not transform my life; rather it empowered my understanding of choice and *The Power of Choice*. The catalyst moment in my life occurred by understanding that in spite of my past experiences, I could powerfully choose, and commit to, a new action anytime. Although the action (showing up) was small, simple and came with discomfort, I powerfully chose it, and that choice led to a world of possibility and a life I love!

If actions lead to results, and new actions lead to new results, consider that action accompanied with a proper understanding of *The Power of Choice*, could lead to unimaginable results! When you understand the power of your choices you become not only equipped to proceed, but powerful in your progress. Understanding your power is especially important since catalyst moments are often presented when things are not going well. They are exposed during times of pain and frustration that are neither ideal nor convenient. For this reason, these moments are often ignored or perceived as a 'bad' idea. But consider this is where breakthrough often sits; on the other side of discomfort, pain, frustration, doubt and fear. And if one does not understand the power of their choices, they may not be equipped to powerfully choose to breakthrough that discomfort.

In my case, breakthrough was on the other side of 'showing up'. While I had to powerfully choose to deal with the initial discomfort that came with the action, the result led to new possibilities that fundamentally transformed my life! In essence, being out of my comfort zone is what eventually became my comfort, and since properly understanding *The Power of Choice*, along with *The Power of Testimony*, I am able to powerfully progress, in spite of discomfort, time and time again.

Consider your 'catalyst moment' is waiting for you on the other side of discomfort, pain, frustration, doubt and fear.

Perhaps you have the desire to change, but find yourself unable to take that first step because you feel stuck. This is likely because you have given your power to your 'reasons'. Every person possesses *The Power of Choice* – the power to choose a new way of being, a new lifestyle, a new hobby, a new look, a new anything. But if you do not understand the power of your choices, you give up your power to your 'reasons'. Where are these reasons you ask? Reasons lie in your most powerful asset; your testimony. The testimony you share about your experiences determines your mindset, which determines your actions and consequently, determines the results in your life. This is why testimonies are powerful (more on that in *The Power of Testimony*).

Consider where you are in your life right now is the result of your actions. If you are not happy with your present status then ask yourself... *Am I utilizing 'The Power of*

Choice' in a way that is serving me? Often, we let our power get consumed by an experience or circumstance which then becomes the 'reason' that we tell ourselves things are not working out and why we are not happy. Consider you create the reason, and give it your power in order to have something to blame so that you will not have to accept responsibility for the results of your actions.

Eventually, I realized that my reason (being the victim) was not serving me, as I perpetually found myself unhappy. And unless I wanted to continue being depressed, I realized I had to change. Although being the victim was the fact, I was letting it be the 'reason' for my result. I was letting 'the victim' have all of my power so that I would have something to blame in order to alleviate myself from being responsible for my depression. I could have chosen to continue letting the victim have my power; blame the result (depression) on the fact that I was a victim of sexual harassment. Instead, I chose to enact my *Power of Choice*. What happened, happened; I was a victim of sexual harassment and that was the fact that I could not change. But what I could change was the power I was giving to the reason, and how I chose to let it affect me. Recognize that I did not powerfully choose to take that first step (showing up) knowing I would instantly be happy. Remember, my catalyst moment presented itself during my peak state of depression and I was very uncomfortable. But, I took a step because I wanted to see if any result, other than the one I was perpetually creating, was possible or available. Sure enough, once I enacted my *Power of Choice* an abundance of possibilities were presented.

Understand that your power is either your greatest strength or your greatest weakness. You, and only you, have the power to change the results of your life. Although you cannot change your experiences, proper understanding of *The Power of Choice* will allow you to enact your power, change your actions, and in turn, change your results. Consider this example:

A woman named Laura claims to be stuck in life because of her weight. When asked about her favorite snack, she responds by saying, *"Potato chips! And I can never have just a few; I have to eat the whole bag!* Laura is then asked, *"Do you realize when you say 'yes' to potato chips you are giving ALL your power to a potato?! A potato is running your life because of the power you are CHOOSING to let it have. Do you believe you are more powerful than a potato?"* To which she replies, *"Yes."* *"Then for seven days choose to be more powerful than a potato and see what happens!"*

Driven by the thought of actively experiencing the results of her actions through *The Power of Choice*, Laura accepts the challenge. For seven days she commits to being attentive of her power and powerfully chooses not to eat potato chips. At the end of the seven days, Laura is glowing with confidence. In choosing to be more powerful than potato chips, she understands her power and in this way, empowers her understanding of choice.

Initially, Laura's testimony emphasized that the 'reason' for her weight was because of genetics; as such, she had no control over the result. After completing *The Seven Day*

Commitment Challenge and enacting *The Power of Choice*, she realized not only were her actions literally feeding the result (her weight), they were also feeding her mindset about genetics. Even if, from a scientific standpoint, genetics proved to be a reason for her weight, she realized genetics did not have to be 'her' reason and therefore, stopped giving genetics her power. When Laura stopped giving all her power to her reasons (potato chips and genetics), the results of her life instantly changed; not necessarily because she instantly lost weight, but because she discovered her power and the immediate impacts one can experience when they understand *The Power of Choice*.

Your beliefs are the filters of your reality. When you surrender an old belief, a new world of possibility is revealed. In becoming aware of your power you become attentive to your choices, and begin to understand that you consistently control the result.

Consider you are on an 'a-maze-ing' journey, which is very much like a maze. Though you may have an idea of the destination, the route is never concrete. All you can ever see is the next few steps ahead and you cannot see around the corner until you take that first step and go around the corner. You develop and grow with each step which is why it is called a journey.

I had no idea that 'showing up' was going to completely transform my life. And had I known the entire journey from the beginning, I would have never left my house since the proceeding steps would have been intimidating and overwhelming. However, completing the first step (showing up) was very important because it gave me confidence. This confidence then allowed me to take the next step and the next step, and so on.

Every step on the path leads to the goal. Even if you do not know the goal, understand that no action goes to waste; including those that seem seemingly insignificant. This book project, for example, is the result of hundreds of thousands of steps. But recognize, that had I undermined the first small simple step and let my discomfort consume me, the project would cease to exist. For this reason, action must be accompanied by proper understanding; for when you understand *The Power of Choice* you become equipped to powerfully and passionately progress on your a-maze-ing journey!

If you are ready to experience the transformational results that occur when you deeply understand *The Power of Choice*, then I invite you to take *The Seven Day Commitment Challenge*. This challenge will assist you in four areas. It will allow you to first, understand the powerful impacts of your choices. Second, consciously experience the impacts of your choices (as you will be aware of your power). Third, allow you to recognize that multiple results are possible and available right now; and fourth, equip you to take that first step in order to progress on the journey of your choosing. If you are ready to produce unimaginable results in your life, turn the page and follow the ten steps which will guide you to complete *The Seven Day Commitment Challenge*.

The Seven Day Commitment Challenge

For this challenge you will need:

- Your daily calendar/ schedule (I recommend using your cell phone to set alerts and reminders).
- If you do not use a cell phone, then a calendar or planner on which you can write will suffice.

Step One: The Commitment

Sit down and think of an area of your life where you are not producing the results you wish to produce or consider a habit you wish to change.

TIP: Choose something meaningful – something that is important to you!

Examples:

A) You own a guitar but never have time to practice.
B) You drink four cups of coffee every day.

Step Two: The Result

Determine the result you wish to produce in this area.

TIP: Keep it simple and be specific!

Examples:

A) I wish to play the song *Happy Birthday* on my guitar.
B) I wish to drink less coffee. Two cups per day.

Step Three: The Plan

Planning is a fundamental part of the commitment process. A plan will serve as an outline for you to follow so you do not revert to your old habits. Consider logistics that need to be addressed in order to bring this commitment to fruition. In order to achieve new results you have to 'do the work' which will require you to be flexible in your schedule; however for this challenge, your commitment should remain straightforward and practical.

TIP: Be detailed in your plan notes!

Examples:

A) I will commit to playing my guitar for 45 minutes. I will practice my guitar every morning, in my room, before work from 7:00-7:45am. I will practice the song *Happy Birthday*.
B) I will drink one cup of coffee in the morning with my breakfast which will take place at 8:00am. I will sit down and enjoy my breakfast and my coffee at the kitchen table. I will drink the second cup of coffee in the afternoon at 2:30pm with a colleague.

Important: While it may seem excessive and unnecessary to plan for a seemingly simple commitment, consider that changing your habits requires specific training which includes a detailed plan.

Step Four: The Schedule

Put your commitment into your schedule. This is where a cell phone is useful since you can set alerts and reminders in your calendar. Schedule your commitment in a designated time slot every day for seven days. If you are not using a cell phone, do the same on your preferred medium and ensure it is posted some place where you will see or have access to it throughout the day.

TIP: Consider possible distractions when scheduling your commitment. Be mindful of the time and the location. Plan how you will deal with possible distractions now!

Examples:

- A) I will tell my family about my guitar practice so that they will not disturb me during this time. I will turn off my cell phone during my 45 minutes of practice.
- B) If I get invited to drink coffee at another time during the day or if I crave another cup of coffee, I will drink warm water instead of coffee.

Important: In addition to scheduling your commitment, block an hour of time in your schedule on day eight. This is your *Commitment Reflection Time (CRT)* in which you will review your week. I suggest scheduling your *CRT* in the morning on day eight.

Step Five: Review

Once you have scheduled your commitment and *CRT*, review the logistics and make sure you have everything that you need for when you start the challenge the following day. Remember, this commitment is important to you! Take the time now to ensure everything is ready so you can truly commit to what you indicated you wish to change in your life.

TIP: Make a check list!

Examples:

A) Do I have the sheet music for the song *Happy Birthday*? Do I need a new guitar pick? Is there a stool in my room to sit on?

B) Is the coffee maker working? Do I have fresh coffee at home? Does the machine have an option to make one cup of coffee at a time?

Step Six: Share

Share your commitment with a friend, family member, colleague, etc. Commitments live in language, and when you put your commitment into words and say it out loud to a person, it becomes real to you and real to them. For the next seven days, not only will your reality include your commitment, but their reality of you will include your commitment.

Important: Sharing your commitment is not done for accountability purposes. If you depend on a person during this challenge, you cannot expect to continue on your own once the seven days are complete. Additionally, if you do not complete the challenge the person with whom you shared may become the reason (the one you blame) for your result. This challenge is training you to be the master of your life through a commitment. By sharing it with a person, you are acknowledging the responsibility you are taking on.

Share: *For the next seven days I am committing to . . . I am sharing this commitment with you because I acknowledge I am solely responsible for the results in my life, and I stand for having an extraordinary life!*

Step Seven: The Seven Day Commitment Challenge

Start your day by saying the following *Commitment Statement* out loud in front of a mirror...

Today is a new day! I am excited for this transformation. This commitment will produce new results and open my life to new possibilities. I am choosing to commit to . . . for seven days because . . .

- I want what is best for my health, my happiness and my life.
- I am ready to explore new opportunities.
- The results in my life are solely based on my actions.
- I have the power to transform my life.
- ...

TIP: Say the statement with confidence and power! If you wish to produce transformation in your life, say the words in a way that you believe them.

Important: Acknowledging yourself, and what you are about to take on, is a very important part of the process. Language exists in reality, and when you see and hear yourself say your commitment in 'reality', it becomes real to you.

Do the work you committed to for the next seven days. Start each morning with the *Commitment Statement*, refer to your plan for guidance and enjoy the process!

Step Eight: Reflect

On day eight, use the hour you scheduled for *CRT* in **Step Four** to reflect on your week.

TIP: Sit in a quiet place where you will not be disturbed. Remember, this is your life, and it is important to you. Take the time now to reflect and take note of your week.

Important: This is not a time to judge or criticize yourself for what you did or did not do; rather, thoughtfully reflect.

Did you complete the commitment as planned?

- If *fully* completed, what did you learn through the process of *fully* committing?
- What did this commitment show you, and contribute to your life?
- What are your reasons?

- If *partially* completed, what did you learn through the process of *partially* committing?
- What interfered with your commitment?
- What are your reasons?

- If *not* completed, what did you learn through the process of *not* committing?
- Why did you not complete the commitment?
- What are your reasons?

- If the commitment *changed*, what did you learn through the *changing* process?
- Where did the commitment lead you?
- What are your reasons?

Step Nine: Consider

The goal of this challenge was to train you to be the master of your life. Mastering your life means that you are self-dependent. You understand that you are solely responsible for your actions (choices) which in turn determine the results you produce in your life. This challenge was designed to develop your awareness of your power. When you understand the power of your choices, you become aware of what you give your power to and as a result, you become aware of your actions.

Consider the result from *The Seven Day Commitment Challenge* foreshadows how you live your life.

- If you *fully* completed the challenge, observe where else in your life you fully complete and commit to things. Consider what results are possible or available through its completion and by being fully committed.

- If you *partially* completed the challenge, observe where else in your life you partially complete and commit to things. Consider what results are or are not possible or available through its partial completion and by being partially committed.

- If you did *not* commit, observe where else in your life you fail to complete and commit to things. Consider what results are not possible or available through not completing and not committing.

Whether you fully committed, partially committed or did not commit, observe in all cases you have reasons; reasons for completing the challenge and reasons for not completing the challenge. Reasons why you were late and reasons why you were on time. Reasons why you chose to eat salad and reasons why you chose to eat a hamburger. In essence, you will always have reasons, but what is important to consider is the power you choose to give to those reasons.

As previously mentioned, your power can be your greatest strength or your greatest weakness. If you do not accept responsibility for your results, that means you are giving your power to your reasons. These reasons are what is overpowering you and preventing you from moving forward and obtaining the results on the journey you desire. When you accept responsibility, you empower yourself. Once you are empowered, you are then equipped to enable, enlighten and enrich the lives of others. But consider it begins with you enacting your power, and *The Power of Choice*.

Choose to be more powerful than your reasons!

Tell yourself... *I am more powerful than . . .*

How empowered do you think Laura felt when she took a stand for her life and declared, '*I am more powerful than potato chips! I am more powerful than genetics in spite of what the science asserts.*' When I chose to be more powerful than my depression, my entire life transformed; I became empowered to be unstoppable and have not stopped since. Consider being responsible and living life on your own terms is an empowering place to lay the foundation for your extraordinary future!

Step Ten: Moving Forward

If you are satisfied with your result from *The Seven Day Commitment Challenge*, refer to *Option A* for next steps. If you are not satisfied with your result, refer to *Option B*.

Option A: If you are satisfied with your result from the challenge, acknowledge what you accomplished in seven days. When you powerfully chose your actions, you produced new results in areas of your life or changed habits that were perhaps a part of your life for some time. No one made you do this challenge, and no one did the work for you. Be proud of the step you took and the work you committed too. By completing this challenge you took a stand for your life, and the result of 'doing the work' led to you experiencing *The Power of Choice* and making powerful progress on your desired journey.

Now that you have completed *The Seven Day Commitment Challenge* and have taken the first step at being the master of your own life, do you understand . . .

1. The powerful impacts of your choices?

2. The impacts you can experience when you become aware of your power and powerfully choose your actions?
3. That multiple results are possible and available right now?

Since you have developed an awareness of your power and begun to understand the responsibility of being the master of your life, here are possible next steps moving forward. You may wish to continue with this commitment or if new possibilities emerged because of the challenge, you may wish to choose a new commitment. Whatever step you powerfully choose, consider there is no 'right' way or 'one' way to live your life, nor can anyone tell you the 'best' way. We are all on our own journeys; there is no race and there is no competition. As such, powerfully choose a step that works for you. The journey is a long process – a life time job – but if you are patient and persistent in your progress, you will no doubt achieve unimaginable results and live an extraordinary life!

Option B: If you are not satisfied with your results from the challenge, acknowledge yourself for considering it. Recognize there is nothing wrong with where you are in life right now. Consider not completing the challenge was a valuable step on your journey.

By not completing *The Seven Day Commitment Challenge* do you understand . . .

1. The powerful impacts of your choices?

2. The impacts you experience when you do not powerfully choose your actions?
3. That by not powerfully choosing your actions, you continue to produce the same results?

Producing new results and changing habits requires that you 'do the work'. No one can do the work for you. Intellectual insights and thought provoking ideas will remain intellectual and thought provoking unless they are applied. You know that actions lead to results; as such, only through practice will you obtain tangible results. Although you did not complete the challenge, that does not mean you cannot commit again. If you wish to proceed with the same commitment, review **Step Two** to **Step Six**. If you wish to choose a new commitment, review **Step One** to **Step Six**.

I invite you to take a stand for your life; get present to your power and experience the unimaginable results that come with doing the work. Powerfully choose to take a step on the journey you desire by re-committing to *The Seven Day Commitment Challenge* and experiencing *The Power of Choice*.

The Power of Testimony

After reading the women's testimonies, you no doubt recognize *The Power of Testimony*. Testimonies are powerful because they are real, raw, and personal. It is the only thing that is truly yours and differentiates you from everyone else in this world. Even if we do not share the same experiences, you find yourself touched and empowered because within a testimony lies a person's voice. The more personal the voice, the more universal it becomes; as such, testimonies connect people because everyone can relate to the universal notion of having had experiences.

At the time of submission, the women in this book faced a lot of unknowns. They had no idea who their testimony was going to impact, the number of people it was going to influence, how people were going to react, and the list goes on. They could have chosen to give their power to their reasons as to why they should not participate; be consumed by their questions, which had no answers, and the fear of embarrassment and judgement that may arise by openly sharing their personal experiences. In spite of their fears, and the fact they will never fully know the impact their testimony will have on a person, each women chose to powerfully step into the unknown and share their lives with the world. While each had their own motives to participate, as a collective they were driven by the projects possibility. Knowing the project and the possibility that their testimony could potentially empower a person existed, made the simple, self-less act of sharing a testimony seem very easy and worthwhile.

Serving others is what enriches our existence and allows us to experience true purposeful fulfillment. What is purpose fulfillment? Essentially, you and I and every person in this world, yearns to make an impact. We desire to enrich the lives of others, and to contribute to the greater good and well being of all human beings. This thirst to make people's lives better is ongoing because it validates our purpose here on earth. We want to be valued, to matter, and to feel as though our presence makes a difference. For example, we experience deep satisfaction when we see the smile of a person; especially when we know we were the cause in the matter. Doing something that benefits others is what provides that purposeful fulfillment. And since enriching lives is beneficial for both the receiver and the giver, we continue ourselves; striving to produce two results with our one action.

While serving others is an important part of living a healthy happy life, you may feel like you lack the time, the money and the resources to contribute and have that powerful impact. You feel that what you have to offer is not enough, and despite your genuine desires, sincere intentions and thirst to matter, you stop yourself from contributing before you even start. Most often, this is because all of your attention is focused on what you lack; what you do not have, what you are not able to contribute, and why it is not enough.

Fortunately, there are no parameters or 'minimum requirements' you must meet in order to have an impact and transform a person. The ability to serve is boundless and unlimited! Instead of dwelling in the world of lack, choose to live in the world of abundance; a world where you consider all that you have to offer right now, is exactly what someone else needs! You do not have to have any thing or be anyone – all that is required is that you share your voice, and this lies in your testimony.

The Power of Testimony provides you with a means to matter, and to contribute to the better world vision we all desire simply by speaking openly and authentically, and sharing your experiences. Each and every person has a testimony that is worthy to be shared and heard. Every testimony is significant and will offer something to be learned from since that experience assisted in moulding you! It supports the notion that every person can have an impact and transform the life of someone else simply through a small action such as sharing a personal testimony. Consider being bold and sharing your experiences could be the gateway to transforming the world!

Additionally, *The Power of Testimony* provides an opportunity to empower and connect with people. Sharing my testimony connected me with people who had also faced hardship, and those connections empowered me to create this collective book project. Ultimately, sharing provided me with the opportunity to completely redefine what I saw possible for myself and my life!

I invite you to join the movement of choosing to live passionately over your past by openly sharing your testimony. Be a part of the new reality where people openly discuss their experiences and acknowledge the beauty of life's journey. Consider your testimony may assist in transforming the lives of others, and your experiences may be exactly what someone else needs to hear in order to move forward and be empowered in their own life.

We all cast our votes by what we choose to do and what we choose not to do. What you do as an individual affects the global environment. There is no such thing as a tiny act, it all matters! And I believe as a collective, we have the power to transform the world, one testimony at a time. As such, if you are ready to experience the powerful effects of your testimony, then I invite you to turn the page, follow *The Guidelines* and join the sharing movement. Remember, your testimony is a souvenir of your experiences. It is what you brought with you to share with the world!

The Guidelines

Each of the women in this book had experiences they struggled with; ones which have shaped their lives, shook their confidence and left them feeling, at one point or another, alone or ashamed. Although I reviewed all the submissions, writing one's own testimony allowed the participants to understand the 'story' in which they were repeatedly telling themselves (perhaps for years) about their experiences.

To live passionately over your past you must first, eradicate defilements and negativities from within. In order to do so, you must invest the time and 'do the work' on yourself; only then will you experience real joy, peace, harmony and happiness. Time does not heal. A person has to be active with their time in order to obtain new results and move forward. As such, you need to actively do the work on yourself in order to change your story into a powerful testimony! No one can do the work for you. You have to work for your own liberation. Additionally, you must work on yourself before you can assist others. Once you do the work, you will be equipped to assist many. The testimonies the women choose to share, along with the life they choose to live, is a direct result of their self-work. Ultimately, you will only ever experience the results of your actions.

Below are *The Guidelines* that were provided to the Passion over Past participants for this book project. You too can start the process of 'doing the work' in order to live passionately over your past. Begin the journey of understanding that your testimony is a catalyst for greatness; not only for your life but for the lives of others as well. Remember, every step on your path matters! Nothing is insignificant. Take a step and see where it leads.

Your testimony should include the following points:

1. Describe briefly the difficulty or the experience.
2. Detail the challenges you faced because of the experience.
3. Describe the 'turning point', transformation or passion in overcoming the experience.
4. Summarize your empowering transformation. (ie. focus on where the transformation has led you and what you are grateful for).
5. Share your testimony passionately with others!

Closing Thoughts

> *Being a visionary means believing in things the rest of us cannot see, and working to make it possible for others to see them.* – Laska Paré

When I started this project, all I had was a vision: A vision of people openly sharing their experiences and empowering each other with their testimony. Once I recognized the powerful effects of *The Power of Choice* and *The Power of Testimony*, I fully committed to this vision. I knew if I could equip a person with this understanding and train them to channel their stories of guilt, anger, resentment, etc., into empowering testimonies, they would not only transform their life, but the lives of others as well.

Transforming the world begins by transforming one person. As such, each person became my goal and as they transformed, I grew one step closer to my vision. Being able to stand for a person's compassion, forgiveness and peace assisted them in truly moving on and living passionately a life of their choosing. Ultimately, this led them to transforming their mindset and being able to not just see, but live their life in a new powerful way!

I truly believe, *if you are passionate and committed, anything is possible!* My passion and commitment to this project has led me closer to my vision, and the possibilities available for the global community. Although the process to achieve my vision was timely, knowing people are empowered, enlightened and enriched in a completely new way made 'doing the work' more exciting and worthwhile.

It is my wish that after reading this book, you will realize that you too can achieve anything; even the unimaginable! Push beyond discomfort and begin the process of living passionately over your past. What are you waiting for? Take that first step and start building an extraordinary life for yourself, your family and others. Remember, hearing intellectual insights and thought provoking ideas are important, but they must be practiced. Only through experience do you truly develop your wisdom. Take action! Share your testimony and exercise your power of choice. Once you do, you will understand that ALL is possible and available right now, including the unimaginable!

I wish you much love, peace and joy on your journey of living passionately over your past. By applying the tools you have learned in this book, you will no doubt be successful!

About the Author

Laska is an international life-coach, a witty blogger and an enthusiastic recreational athlete. When not enabling people with the tools to build better lives for themselves and the global community, you will find her outside seeking adventure! As a life-long learner, Laska is constantly raising her standards and expanding her limits in order to exemplify this notion of endless possibility. She believes sharing provides access for us to see and discover a new layer within ourselves and through compassion and love, we can achieve the greater world vision we all desire.

Visit, share and comment at: www.LaskaPare.com

Additional Information

The Participants: While all contributions were reviewed by the author, each submission was written and submitted by the participant – many of whom consider English their second or third language. For the publication, the participants had the choice to use their real name, remain anonymous, or use another name if they desired. In some instances, names of people and places were changed in order to protect the identity of the participants and those in their testimonies.

The Cover Art: One's path in life is said to be akin to that of the Lotus. Beginning as a seedling, through to the bud emerging from the muddy waters, blooming upon awakening. A powerful symbol of triumph and a renewal of life: Passion over Past.

> *The essence of all beings is Earth. The essence of the Earth is Water. The essence of Water is plants. The essence of plants is the human being.*

> *Esam bhuntanam prthivi rasha, prthivya apo raso-pam osadhayo rasa, osadhinam puruso rasah.*

~ *Chandogya Upanishad I.1.2.* ~

The cover art was designed and donated by Harmony Pillon. Harmony is an interdisciplinary artist working with concepts of herbalism, ecology, plant spirit medicine and Ayurveda; focusing on evolving identities, the temporality of environments, hyperconsciousness and sustainable living processes. The majority of her work focuses on awareness initiatives, seed saving, wild crafting and primitive skill-building. She regards travel as an integral part of this work, immersing oneself in the adventure of the unknown by putting energy into other ways of living, stepping back and recognizing the simplicities of life.

You may connect with Harmony at pillonhr@gmail.com and www.HarmonyPillon.com

Stay Connected: Connect with the community of those choosing to live passionately over their past through our social media.

- Facebook.com/PassionOPast
- Twitter: @PassionOPast

Acknowledgments

To the book participants: Your courage to accept and embrace life's experiences and share them for the highest good of others is truly an expression of unconditional love!

Each of you has touched and enlightened my life in a very special way. I am so grateful for your contribution to the book and in awe of your commitment to inspire others. From the bottom of my heart, THANK YOU! Thanks for believing in my vision which we, as a collective, have made a reality!

To Radamis: You supported the idea of me creating 'something' long before this project was conceived. Your assistance throughout the entire process was uncanny! Your confidence in me allowed this project to blossom. Thank you for reminding me of my voice. I am sincerely grateful for your dedication and commitment.

To Amar: I greatly appreciated all your support with this project. You constantly had your ears open and eyes peeled; networking and connecting me with relevant opinion leaders and organizations. Thank you for being the inquisitive, loving person that you are – always honest and unlimited in your sharing.

To Ashutosh: Thank you for providing me with a space to pursue my passions. Your generosity and hospitality in India allowed me to stay focused and on track, while the laughter and jokes kept me gratefully entertained! Your assistance enabled me to equip others, and for that, I am deeply grateful!

To my fabulous Uncle Christian: Your commitment to both me and this project is beyond what I can express in words. Your mentorship has transformed my entire way of being. You believed in me before I believed in myself and because of your guidance, I got present to my purpose and obtained the confidence to pursue it passionately!

Made in the USA
Charleston, SC
25 June 2015